MEN I HOLD GREAT

FRANÇOIS MAURIAC

MEN I HOLD GREAT

KENNIKAT PRESS
Port Washington, N. Y./London

Translated from the Original French
Mes Grands Hommes
by ELSIE PELL

MEN I HOLD GREAT

Copyright, 1951, by Philosophical Library
Reissued in 1971 by Kennikat Press by arrangement
Library of Congress Catalog Card No: 78-132088
ISBN 0-8046-1416-4

Manufactured by Taylor Publishing Company   Dallas, Texas

ESSAY AND GENERAL LITERATURE INDEX REPRINT SERIES

CONTENTS

	PAGE
Pascal	1
Molière the Tragic	11
Voltaire Versus Pascal	24
Jean-Jacques Rousseau	30
I. The Confessions	
II. The Solitary Wanderer	
Chateaubriand	61
Maurice and Eugénie de Guérin	66
Balzac	77
Gustave Flaubert	85
Loti	105
Barrès	109
I.	
II. The Judges of Barrès	
A Brief Case for André Gide	117
Radiguet	120
Graham Greene	124
Index	129

PASCAL

O N THE TABLE, WITHIN REACH OF MY HAND, I SEE THE
scholarly edition of the *Pensées et Opuscules*,[1] published by Hachette with introduction, reviews, notes and
two facsimiles of the manuscript of the *Pensées*, by Monsieur
Léon Brunschvicg. That little book, dragged about with
me everywhere since I was in the fifth grade, dog-eared, yel-
lowed, filled with notes, thumb-prints, photographs, dates,
dried petals, like those books spoken of by Rimbaud "which
had dipped in the ocean"—closed and to all appearances dead
in times of folly and distractions—came to life once more,
opened up again, on certain evenings, along with my soul,
and with the return of my thirst, the spring bubbled up anew.

Monsieur Pierre Lasserre assures me that, during his last
inner struggles before leaving Saint-Sulpice, Renan went to
Pascal for help and that, for the moment, he hoped the
author of the *Pensées* would save him. What Pascal could
not do for Renan, he succeeded in doing for some of us who
were not, to be sure, philosophers. He intervened in our
destiny at a time when the adolescent, succeeding the devout
and credulous child, leaves the nest, full of excitement, and
suddenly discovers the twofold universe of knowledge and
passion. Before any philosophical or sensuous reading, before
amorous experience, he breathes in the wind what he does

---

[1] *Thoughts and Short Works.* Trans. Note.

1

not yet know, and certain images strike him, predispose him
to denial. On one hand, he thinks he sees a mumbling flock
of women, all the hideousness, all the wretchedness, the intellectual poverty, base credulity, hatred, the fear of strange,
alluring passions and, under the guise of edification, prejudice
against the most noble works in favor of false and foolish
rhapsodies; on the other hand, the young professors who are
admired, the famous writers, their daring thoughts, eager
curiosity, unbridled searching and a rightful share granted
the exigencies of the heart. At the very moment when the
choice of an adolescent falls on an impression or on images,
his meeting with Pascal may be decisive; every kind of
grandeur in a single man, and none other than a Christian!

As early as 1684 Bayle wrote, "Free-thinkers can no longer
tell us that only small minds are capable of pity, for we can
point out to them a very well-developed one in one of the
greatest geometricians, one of the most subtle metaphysicians,
and one of the most penetrating minds that has ever lived."

What is most repugnant in the renunciation of some people
is that they possess nothing to give up. Christianity attracts
a host of those who believe that the Gospels authorize them
to glory in their nothingness. And the thing by which it can
be recognized that the Church is not temporal is the reception it gives to the apparent scoffing of the world (apparent,
because some of them attain holiness, and so conceal an
invisible grandeur under their visible poverty). But as for
passionate youths, in love with carnal strength, that miserable
horde around the Christ repels them; that is the moment when
Blaise Pascal can save them, especially if they see him as
he really was, before his final conversion: entirely different
from them in spirit and in knowledge, but their brother in
intellectual pride and even by a certain attraction that the
passions had for him.

Have not the so-called "worldly" periods in the life of this philosopher-mathematician, friend of Fermat, the Duke de Roannez and of the Chevalier de Méré, admired by the whole of Europe at twenty years of age, been reduced over-much? Specialists have gone to a great deal of trouble to make us doubt that the *Discours sur les Passions del Amour* [1] was by Pascal. Even if the material reasons for believing in the authenticity of those admirable pages did not appear to us of the strongest, it would suffice to read them to establish our certainty, so clearly is Pascal revealed in every sentence and so clearly do we recognize that inimitable accent. That young scholar is worldly enough to dedicate his arithmetical machine to the Queen of Sweden in a letter in which is displayed a passionate intellectual pride. He belongs to the world enough to haggle with his sister Jacqueline over the dowry she claims the right to give to Port-Royal; that is because the high society which he enjoys frequenting puts him into embarrassing financial straits.

When speaking of him to Jacqueline, Mother Angélique said that he was "in vanity and pleasure." Did that Pascal of 1652 love or did he merely discuss love? To be sure many people know this passion only by hearsay—many, but not great souls certainly. What great soul has not loved and suffered? Pascal tells us magnificently that "in a great soul everything is great." And after his famous outburst on the life that commences with love and ends with ambition, he adds: "A tumultuous life is acceptable to great minds, but mediocre people take no pleasure in it." Pascal senses his own greatness to the point of writing the Queen of Sweden, at the same time, that the power of kings over their subjects is only an image of the power of the mind over inferior minds. No one could be more persuaded of the superiority of his mind

---

[1] *Discourse on the Passions of Love.* Transl. note.

than he, and he shows it in many a passage "with his usual frankness and simplicity" (he himself uses those expressions in a letter to Madame Périer) .

Now Pascal, with his great soul, does not seem to believe that a great soul can remain ignorant of love; for that great tumultuous life that is pleasing to great minds is also, so he assures us, "a marvelous step toward passion." According to him, the tumult of a fine life possesses an incomparable power of seduction: "A stormy life surprises, strikes and penetrates." This word is worthy of the Grande Mademoiselle or of the Coadjutor. Besides, here you have Pascal's confession: "It is useless to hide, one loves always." Mere rhetoric, they say. But how could a hearsay acquaintance with love furnish Pascal with light on that passion such as no other in his time possessed? It is certain that he foresaw all the subtleties that please modern authors in their analyses. Before Barrès' *Homme libre,* Pascal knew that what increases the pleasure of exaltation greatly is its analysis, and that it is necessary to feel as deeply as possible while analyzing as much as possible. Pascal knew it when he wrote: "Clarity of mind causes clarity of passion also. That is why a great, clear mind loves with ardor and sees distinctly what it loves." Pascal felt instinctively that it is ourselves that we look for in others, and that we create the object of our passion with our own substance: "Man must find within himself the model of that beauty for which he is searching outside . . ." He was not ignorant of the fact that we do not fall in love with beauty, but a certain beauty in conformity with our standard; and it is in this sense that it can be said everyone has the original of the beauty whose copy he is looking for in the wide world. He knew perfectly what Proust called "the intermittences of the heart," as these astonishing lines prove: "Attachment to the same thought wearies and destroys the

mind of man. That is why it is sometimes better for the se-
curity of love's delight for one not to know he loves; and that
is not being unfaithful, for one does not love anyone else; it is
renewing one's strength to love better. That is done so much
that one thinks of it . . ." And at length he proclaimed the
tyranny of love: "It is a tyrant that will not suffer a companion; it wishes to be alone; all the passions must yield and
obey it." Pascal dared to make the statement that a novelist,
forced to paint the realities of love, would have to put into
his works in a footnote: "Passion knows no limits."

Would it have been sufficient to have studied love from
the outside to get acquainted with it so quickly? Certain
passages in the *Discours,* less surprising and more familiar,
certainly betray tender experiences: on the resolutions that
one makes to do and say certain things when the loved one is
there, but whose presence upsets all our plans; on the perpetual novelty that we experience in that presence which is
a *cessation of anxiety* (three hundred pages of Proust are
contained in those three words). To be sure, no one who knows
Pascal can deny him a nature capable of storms, according
to the expression of Sainte-Beuve. But must one admit
straight off with Sainte-Beuve that Pascal exhausted those
storms in the sphere of science and in religious distress?

On the other hand, aside from Mademoiselle de Roannez
whom he guides as Monsieur Singlin would do, and the
affected ladies of Clermont to whom, according to Fléchier,
Pascal showed marked attention, no woman of the world is
apparent in his life. On looking at the *Discours* more closely,
certain less passionate passages, which demonstrate some
experience, could have been inspired in Pascal by mere friendship. As different as are the two sentiments in their nature,
they have nevertheless some characteristics in common. Now
the seventeenth century seems to us to be truly the *Mono-*

motapa of friendship. Society life, the custom well-bred people had of putting all their findings in common, of informing
each other of their reading and occupations, the means of
transportation so precarious that they introduced into the
slightest separations that anxiety and distress expressed in
the fable of the *Two Pigeons*, the long epistolary exchanges,
the endless civilities of the language of that day which neces-
sarily ended by awakening the sentiments of which they had
at first been only an end—all that developed friendship won-
derfully, and lent to it delicacy which, without ever confusing
it with a more lively sentiment, could help Pascal imagine
certain phases of it. So what he writes of the presence and
absence of the Duke de Roannez who was so attached to
him "that he got along so ill without him that he took him
with him in his administration of Poitou" . . . (Marguérite
Périer). At the time of his final conversion, Jacqueline and
Monsieur Singlin thought it best to send Pascal away from
Paris "so as to be more alone than he was due to the return
of his friend, the Duke of Roannez, who took up all his time.
He entrusted his secret to him, and with his consent, which
was not given without tears, left the day after Epiph-
any . . ." (Letter from Jacqueline to Madame Périer.)

How far we are from the frightening genius, the sublime
misanthrope of the histories of literature! "The delightful and
guilty use of the world," he wrote in his *Prayer for the good
use of illnesses*. This is how Polyeuctus characterizes sensual-
ity: delightful source. Pascal gave up, but did not close his
eyes to those delights. His heart, capable of storms like every
young heart, open perhaps to love, but certainly to pride,
and sensitive to friendship, does nothing more when he is
converted, than turn this infinite power of feeling toward the
Infinite Being. How pathetic is that supreme meeting of the
Abbé Ernest Renan with Pascal, whose traces Pierre Lasserre

has rediscovered! Pascal has, indeed, destroyed in advance the obstacles that Renan piled up between his soul and God. Renan writes somewhere that he would be glad to ascend the stairway of Santa Casa on his knees, if they did not want to force him to admit the messianic interpretation of such and such a psalm. Pascal could have taught him that it is not texts which give God to us, and that He is not the reward of the philologists. But, one will say, the science of exegesis was not very far advanced in Pascal's time. Perhaps if he had been acquainted with the works of Strauss, Harnack and Loisy . . . well, if he had known them, he would have repeated what he said to Madame Périer, that: "The Holy Scriptures are not a science of the mind, but a science of the heart which is intelligible only to those who have an upright heart, and that the others sense only the darkness." To be sure, he does not deny the miracles or the prophecies, but he accords them so little importance for the faith that they inspire this terrible witticism: "You think that (the prophecies) are related to make you believe? No, it is to keep you from believing." And again: "The miracles are not used as a means of conversion but of condemnation." Here the Jansenist betrays himself. But to sum it all up, since there are so many unbelievers, that is the evidence that miracles and prophecies are not conclusive proofs and that they have little more practical value to overcome doubt "than the course of the moon and the planets" whose misuse by so many apologists Pascal finds so ridiculous. "That gives them the right (the unbelievers) to think that the proofs of our religion are pretty weak." What does Pascal bring to us which permits him to show himself so scornful of traditional proofs? But right here, let us put, in its proper place, the argument of the "pari" [1] which, because it is most

[1] The famous "bet" of Pascal. Transl. note.

fully developed in the manuscript of the *Pensées,* is offered to
his opponents as a convenient cynosure. To tell the truth, the
apologetics of Pascal are based so little on it that it could be
said they exist entirely without it. This argument tends only
to shake us out of our indifference. The essence of Pascal is
elsewhere. In brief, the author of the *Pensées* establishes between Christianity and man the relationship of a key to its
lock. Man with his complexity, Christianity with its complexity, fit perfectly into each other. "Not a dogma, one
might say, that does not stop up one of our chasms, which
does not fill them to capacity." A demonstration that is of
value in proportion as the image of man that we are shown
will not be manipulated by the cause. But rightly speaking,
no one before Pascal and no one after him was able to draw
with a few simple and eternal strokes that relief map of man,
with its summits and hollows. Yet Voltaire objects to Pascal
on the grounds that it is not enough for a religion to explain
man for us to consider it as a revealed one. To be sure! but
that is enough for us to wish it to be so. And just as Pascal
has established the relationship between Catholicism and us
by using his reason, so it is first to our reason that he appeals.

It is true that we do not attain God through reason alone.
And so, let's incline the automate, stupefy ourselves! Odious
suggestion that suddenly makes the sublime word burst out:
"to offer oneself to inspirations through humiliations." Now
the bridge has been let down from the bank where passionate
reason had led us to the other bank where love awaits us.
Here Pascal hands us what Rimbaud calls: "the key to the
ancient banquet . . ." Charity is that key.

Why have they spoken of the quivering and terrified genius
of Pascal? For what man has known tranquil love better? It
seems as though he was spared every obscure darkness of

the mystics. To no other heart was God more perceptible. Pascal escapes the darkest side of Jansenism because he knows he is preferred, he knows he is chosen. On the night of November 23 he receives confirmation of it, that night with its tears of joy, with its unshadowed certainty, its total and sweet renunciation and its peace. And as though the words of his God were not sufficient which, through Pascal, still reach and burn us: "You would not look for Me if you had not already found Me . . . I have loved you more deeply than you have loved your blemishes . . ." here to fill him completely is the cure of the little Périer by the contact alone of the Sacred-Thorn. So in spite of his Jansenism, Pascal bore in his sick and suffering heart, the most joyous soul: "I am as happy" wrote Jacqueline to him, "to find you gay in your solitude as I was unhappy when I saw you were so in the world. Yet I don't know how Monsieur de Sacy adapts himself to so joyful a penitent . . ." Pascal, the joyful penitent, writes to Mademoiselle de Roannez that the sufferings of Christians "are not without pleasure and are overcome only by pleasure." He warns her not to think "that piety consists only of bitterness without consolation." What holy delight bursts out in that fine Jansenist expression: "The victorious delectation of grace!"

But once in possession of this happiness, Blaise Pascal paid with everything on which the world puts its highest price: pleasure would be nothing, but the sciences, in which he showed remarkable genius; why even the most legitimate tenderness, for he went so far in his scruples as to rebuff his sisters, and he did not want anyone to love him: "It is not right for anyone to attach himself to me . . . I would deceive those in whom I should awaken desire, for I am no one's end . . ."

The young man who had followed him until then, at this moment turns and goes away, sad: the word almost impossible to pronounce, if not with the lips at least with the heart, is the one that opened the kingdom of joy to Pascal: "Lord, I give You all."

MOLIÈRE THE TRAGIC

MOLIÈRE, THE SHARP-TONGUED, THE DEPRESSED, THE PROfound Molière takes up Pascal's challenge. He dares to bet against Pascal. Not that he denies the supernatural; but he refuses to be bothered with it, and finds a man who worries about his soul comical. The Imaginary Invalid is not Argan alone, a prey to apothecaries, but also the pious Orgon with whom the gentle Tartuffe is living. Even if he were not his dupe, and if that saintly man of a Tartuffe were steeped in true devotion, in Molière's eyes, Orgon would be ridiculous just the same.

The pious people of the Court and city were quite right not to trust the tirades against false and true devotion by which Molière tried to sidetrack them. For the character of Tartuffe is not the one that separates us; humanists and devout agree on laughing him to scorn. But the orchestra would not have the heart to laugh at Orgon if he were only a just man exploited by a rascal. He is a passionate Christian; and so, according to Molière, as grotesque as those who do not know how to be moderate in all things. It matters little to Molière to know whether Orgon understands Christianity well or badly. Molière, if he were logical, would have to turn every precept of Christ's into derision, because it shocks nature. To tell the truth, if he doesn't dare do it directly, he succeeds

11

with Orgon, the clumsy disciple, in whom the most sublime passion is expressed by a simper.

Molière wishes to recognize only his instinct, an instinct that fear of ridicule alone restrains. That is what he calls nature. From his early days in Paris and during his first trips through France, he pursues an instinctive life, yields to every passion offered. Madeleine Béjart is dear to him. Is there anything more simply human than to satisfy his amorous inclination, anything that deserves less to be taken tragically? Without doubt it is also the most commonplace thing for Madeleine Béjart to give birth to a little girl, that this child should grow up, and that Molière, consumed with work and pleasure, in the course of his blazing life, should find still more beauty in her than he had loved in her mother.

Ramon Fernandez tells us that Molière "deeply rooted in nature and sensuous life," could renew himself only in a new woman. Had there been the slightest shadow of a doubt as to the origin of that little Armande, had there been only one chance that she was of his blood, a man less determined than Molière not to dramatize life, would perhaps have abstained. He would have perceived that nature is not so simple, nor so good; and that feelings, the most pure outwardly, sometimes deviate. Without a doubt, Molière had seen the birth of the little Armande; but in his place, the stupid Orgon himself would have perceived at once a disturbing attraction being born in his heart. That is because the half-witted Orgon believes, like Pascal, that nature is corrupt. What do I say: believes? It is not a question of believing this truth, but of seeing it. It is not only a matter of faith: one has only to open his eyes. Nature is corrupt, you see it very well. And if you have sufficient hypocrisy to deny it, you show that corruption all the more "by such unnatural feelings"; and moreover, now you are as ridiculous as Sganarelle who does not wish to be the age he is: you do not want to have the nature that you have.

So this great honest man Molière (and I do not write that by antiphrasis), by having claimed to follow nature alone, finds himself, in the eyes of his century, suspected of incest. His last biographer, without accusing him clearly of the crime, is even more careful not to absolve him of it. Nothing but his instinct led Molière to this extremity, where he persuaded himself that he had only obeyed temperate and smiling reason while he did not even obtain "the delightful and guilty usage of the world" of which Pascal speaks, but a guilty and atrocious use. Until their death, the destinies of Armande and Molière remain intertwined, without her being able to give him even one drop of the love for which he thirsts. He says nothing, does nothing that does not repel Armande, when he wishes to get closer to her. His deep instinct, at every instant, is spoiled by his stiff and clumsy will.

Molière is sad, much sadder than Pascal. Jacqueline Pascal disputed with her brother, and asked him jokingly what Monsieur Singlin would think of so joyful a penitent. Pascal's tears of joy do not appear during the "night of fire"; only there is scarcely any "thought" on which the Christian's happiness does not touch lightly.

The taciturnity of Molière struck all his contemporaries. This opponent of Christians who cast a shadow over earthly life, this friend of the natural and reasonable world who made the court laugh at the expense of unlimited virtue, was himself a gloomy man. This humanist makes fun of extreme Christians because they seem to believe incompatible the earth and the sky, a worldly life and a life of grace. But he? All his existence proves the strange incompatibility between what he wishes and what he realizes; he lacks both wisdom and happiness. This contemner of every vice moves in an atmosphere of crime; and this partisan of felicity made to measure and well balanced, eats his heart out in solitary and despairing passion.

The choice must be made between relying on instinct or relying on grace. At the signal of instinct, Molière's destiny turns black; he gets a laugh from the others; but he himself weeps off stage before dying. In the whole seventeenth century, there is not a passage that gives forth a more painful sound than Molière's confidences to Chapelle: one of those too human cries, coming too directly from the very heart of a being for us to be able to believe them invented. Knowing he was betrayed, Molière at first sets about conquering himself: "For that I used all my strength of mind." But he confesses that the presence alone of Armande, who is not even beautiful, destroys all his philosophy in an instant. And then, he suddenly falls as low as possible: it is not enough to close his eyes when Armande suffers because of another man: "My passion reached the point of entering into her interests with compassion"; and suddenly this confession makes one tremble on recalling the suspicions and jokes of the world at his expense: "You will tell me doubtless that it is necessary to be a father to love in this way; but, as for me, I believe there is only one kind of love . . ."

A significant word from which Proust's work, in our days, is not sufficient to squeeze out all meaning. Molière might add: "Is not that the height of folly!" Folly, indeed; and of all the follies, the most foolish. How far we are here from the middle ground, the moderation and the balance recommended by humanism. To be truthful, which one, Molière or Pascal, is the victim of a myth? Does temperate nature exist? And is not every man the prey of fearful forces that no one in the world has followed with impunity?

In this matter, the half-witted Orgon could go back to
Molière, if the disorderly and very human taste that he has
for Tartuffe did not make him forget what the catechism
teaches him touching the corruption of nature. Orgon is absurd in proportion as he lacks Christian common-sense:
"Good sense does not weigh much," says Chesterton, "when-
ever the Christian is not there to protect it." Orgon has Tartuffe on the brain, and the more he yields to that attraction
the more he withdraws from Christianity as is proven by that
rascally lesson he recites devoutly, and in which we wonder
that Ramon Fernandez is able to see an exact expression of
Christian doctrine:

> One who acts up to his own precepts enjoys profound
>   peace,
> And looks upon the whole world as so much dirt.

. . . .

> And I could see my brother, children, mother and wife
>   die
> Without troubling myself in the least about it.

Remarks so opposed to Christianity that there is scarcely
need to indicate they express exactly the contrary from it:
the first thing from which Christ delivers us is indifference to our neighbor. How can Ramon Fernandez discover in this the soul of a wholly Christian man? Orgon falls
into a state of insensibility and violates his civic duty; this
mediocre Christian gets his reward in aping the heroic virtue
of souls whose vocation it is to surpass nature. Even Pascal,
who did not want Madame Périer to caress her children too
much, wrote: "I have a heart full of tenderness for those
with whom God has closely united me." So the most austere
of Christians, because he had in a certain manner to cross

over man to reach God, can give witness that nothing human is strange to him.

On the other hand, Molière refuses to pick up the trails in man which would lead him where he does not wish to go. Such rank obstinacy costs him dear: "We lose taste for ourselves," writes Ramon Fernandez, "when we have to give up bringing about in our nature the unity that is in our minds. If Molière was led to recognize the fatality of the senses and the impotence of reason, in the depths of his heart, he did not consent to it."

To avenge himself for a set-back he believes irremediable, it is he and not Pascal who scoffs at man and misrepresents life. Or rather, as in almost all of his comedies, he suppresses the grandeur and shows only the poverty and baseness; or, as in *The Misanthrope*, he turns over humiliated grandeur to the mockery of the world. Pascal's Christian common-sense puts back into synthesis everything in man that Molière divides and disassociates; he recreates our unity, not within us, but beyond us.

To be sure, Molière does not look so far. He runs breathlessly, urged ahead by nuisances and enemies, full of a terrible suspicion, hanging onto the favor of a king who is already turning a little from his dear comedian and beginning to prefer Lulli to him; more alone in love than any man ever was, consumptive, exhausted with work and excesses, he takes good care to teach us how to live! He avenges himself; he turns into derision the precious school, marquis, doctors, devout, the nuisances of all sorts who delay his course; and above all he makes fun of himself; he consoles himself for the distaste that is perhaps given to him every morning in his mirror by the graybearded physiognomy that could be fine and noble in a different lighting than that of carnal passion, his head of an Arnolphe or of a Sganarelle. Molière puts his ludicrous despair out to pasture for the king, the court and the city; a man who loves without being loved makes the very gestures that can do him the most disservice. How comical is his absurd and perhaps guilty passion! It relieves him to make laughter out of such misery. He does not complain himself: why didn't he remain faithful to temperate and pleasing reason! He tells himself, perhaps, that ridicule is the only sanction for our faults. In his eyes, we have to render an account only to the world. And it is the laughter of the world that punishes and absolves us at the same time. When we have laughed hard at the *Miser*, he does not seem horrible to us any more; nor Alceste so ridiculous to claim nobility with the weakest of hearts, and to confuse so easily what shocks virtue with what unleashes jealousy. The contradictions in the character of the *Misanthrope* had at first struck Pascal; but Molière takes no account of them. He bears within him the virtuous compulsion of Alceste, and he is also Armande Béjart's husband, the interested flatterer of an adulterous young king. What does that contradiction mean? What can we deduce from it? For that is just the question. Nothing matters for Molière but survival, or as one says to-day "sticking it out."

"If you were like me," he said to Chapelle, "taken up with pleasing the king, and if you had forty or fifty persons who don't understand reason, to maintain and conduct, a theatre to support, works to accomplish in order to enhance your reputation, you would have no desire to laugh, I assure you. . . ."

In what way, we wonder, does that life of Molière appear to us less tragic, more temperate, more reasonable than Pascal's? Pascal's pangs have become a proverb, but why not Molière's pangs? Whatever side we take in the famous bet to which Pascal drives us, does one seem less heavy with consequences than the other? To search, aside, the meaning of life; to retire from the hurly-burly of the world to reflect on life, even humanly, is that a much more foolish game than to burn up one's life? Pascal, while remaining fully himself, would have been able, moreover, to remain in the world. Besides, did he ever leave it altogether? His illness was his retreat. There are, much more than one would be able to believe, dreamers on the march; men and women who neglect none of their civic duties, and who yet do not cease to live in close union with the living truth within them.

Does not the very nature that Molière defends, honors and violates at every minute, incline us, invite us soon to retreat, reflection and purity? There are many contradictory ways of displeasing nature, and mystics violate their bodies less than do sensuous people. The great ancients before Christ understood that. As we grow older everything happens as though nature were obliging us to detach ourselves more and more from the intoxication of the senses, and to grow more and more in spirit. Is not the sickness, of which Pascal dares to write that it is the habitual state of the Christian, in varying degrees the habitual state of most men? A man over forty years of age, even in relative equilibrium, notices in himself signs and whispering invitations to take care. Blessed, moreover, is he who benefits from those warnings! Many strong men who are warned by nothing, go on and exhaust themselves in every kind of excess until suddenly, they collapse.

Molière, like Pascal, was always ill. If we believe his last biographer, his illness, tuberculosis, was one of those of which men are accustomed to make the worst use. But we doubt that if he had felt the terrible headaches and the intestinal pains that Pascal suffered, and if he had been obliged like him to "purge himself every other day for three months," he would have felt any more curiosity about metaphysics. Which one, then, gives proof of the greater common-sense:

the man who, neither in his doctrine nor in his conduct takes
account of the signs of weakening that he observes in his own
flesh; or the one who considering sickness, aging, decrepitude
and death as given facts, looks for their meaning and, if he
thinks he has found it, applies himself to making good use
of them?

It is a strange injustice to have a grievance against the
Christian because of the feeling he has of his own poverty,
and to accuse him of being weak because he knows he is so.
There is no courage in not knowing oneself; but there is a
great deal in looking oneself in the face. And yet the world
continues to proclaim the sincerity of the carnal minded because they are in accord with their instinct, and to denounce
the lie (they sometimes say "the sublime lie") of beings who
listen to the call of purity and perfection within them.

Is this attraction less our own than that instinct? The
answer is, perhaps, that a more moderate way exists, without
falling into Molière's disorders or Pascal's excesses, and that
an honest man can take his stand between them. That is just
the side that Molière recommends to us, although every day
of his life, he withdraws a little more from it. We should know
if others have succeeded where that great man failed; and if
the golden mean is not just a myth for natures that bear
within them a passionate compulsion. It is up to everyone to
question himself, to look into himself and round about himself. After forty years of age, a man stands in the thick of an
ending battle, of a charnel house, all this decay that still
breathes! Certain living people seem more dead to him than
many dead people he has loved. Someone cries out to us:
"Accept decay; that is perhaps true courage. You see very
well you are afraid, that you need a refuge, a shelter and a
hope on the threshold of death. As in the times of the old
Lucretius, it is always fear that creates the gods."

No, it is not through weakness that we follow the Christ, although we agree. He helps our weakness. Nor is it through fear of death. But, without blushing for it, we trust in the assurance given us that we shall die in His arms! Beforehand the vision tranquilizes our journey—of that God who gives himself to the body about to become only ashes—like a friend who stays behind us in the deserted house, and yet whom we find again at the end of the voyage.

But those who do not have that assurance? What Sainte-Beuve says of life: "A game that must always be lost," is no more true than the contrary proposition: a life is always, in some way, a success, provided that, as Fernandez tells us in his book on *Personality*, "it makes a picture." One would not want to touch up Verlaine's destiny, or even Oscar Wilde's, so satisfying for the mind is the curve. "There is no disorder there for no order has been broken," writes Ramon Fernandez. "In this domain, Molière is on a level of instinctive life, with no impression of fall and with no real fall."

The question could not be stated better. And who will decide between us? We follow the outer curve of a life, what appears of it outside. Often what we see allows us to risk conjectures touching the inner life and what has reference to its relationships with God, and the rule of conduct. Invisible resistances, victories and defeats are visibly inscribed on the apparent destiny. That is true for a great many men. As they advance, they become visibly soiled. On that face, molded by social discipline, profession or the world, the pus slowly oozes out until suddenly, something happens: "Something has to happen, something else . . ." Oscar Wilde's last word, in Algeria, on the eve of the trial in which he will be beaten. It is not always hard labor, but the annoyance of the police, drugs, the asylum, suicide, or a suspicious death, and the world sees a made-up "cadaver" coming back to it, arising from some underworld or other.

Such beings are the cowards, the defeated will say. To be exact, the strength of a man appears in the balance he creates between those two lives. There is, perhaps, as much danger in putting the infinite into intellectual scruples; in loading up the most simple acts with boundless consequences, as to give oneself up, an inert prey, to sensations. Why dramatize Molière? Ultimately, he had a fine destiny. Molière triumphs with an immortal work, with a life whose nobility Fernandez succeeds in showing and, finally, with a death that in the eyes of posterity, Bossuet's anathema does not strip of its grandeur.

Here is where the questionable role of art appears: the work-alibi, the work-excuse. The world makes every existence legitimate, even the worst, if it is ever expressed in a work. The savagery of the world! So much the better that Proust, almost his whole life, suffocated within cork-lined walls. Without that, we should never have had *Remembrance of Things Past*. That passionate, weary Molière, who gives himself up to the theatre, should perhaps have suffered even still more; for a life to make a picture, that should be enough for us; but for a picture to be fixed in a work that future ages will applaud, that is what ends by satisfying the unbiased mind.

Is there anything more tragically inhuman than this game in which we are at the same time both spectators and protagonists? Everyone supplies his race, turns around or jumps over the obstacles, utters cries stupid or meriting to be restrained, before the final hole, before the shovelful of earth over his head. Molière is already half dead when he still exerts every nerve to hold the attention of a king more difficult to amuse. As for his love, he expects nothing more from

it, struggles no more, closes his eyes. Because he has to love
always, he attaches himself, as to a friend, a son or an heir, to
Baron, the prodigal son who, under the features of the shep-
herd of *Mélicerte*, disturbs many hearts, and perhaps
Armande's. But Molière does not feel that any more: he ends
his life beyond all suffering, lost in a sort of despairing peace.

That does not prevent his being out of breath now: "On
the seventeenth of February, as he was giving signs of great
lassitude, he said to his wife and Baron: 'As long as my life
was interwoven with pain and pleasure, I thought I was
happy; but to-day when I am weighed down by cares without
being able to count on a single moment of satisfaction and
ease, I see well that I have to give up the game; I can no
longer hold up against the pain and unpleasantness that do
not give me a moment of relaxation.' "

The comedy is ended. He played well; he can be satisfied.
Everything was for the world, for the distraction and pleasure
of the world. And the world is quits toward him by the memory of his work and name that it will retain. Does he expect
anything else? Fear anything else? Hope anything else? But
no time should be lost in examining conjectures or what is
unverifiable . . .

How human the relentless Pascal appears to us! He recalls
to us that we should not despair too soon; should not decide
accidentally and without reflection. A humanist too, he con-
sents, at the beginning, to consider only the basic facts, the
human element; the conjectures which he hazards, are not up
in the air. Nothing more down to earth than Pascal, in his
first effort. He arises from that same mud with which
Molière has cemented his works; from that heart of which
he dares to write that it was hollow and full of refuse.
Molière, in his old age, no longer believes that anything can
resist that muddy flow, no dike: neither temperate reason,

nor the rules of society, nor the fear of ridicule. The tragic Molière sees nothing any more but an immense disaster. But now on the verge of death, unknown to himself, he bears witness against himself; a single word, uttered spontaneously from his heart, suddenly picks up that frightful and grotesque humanity that he has humiliated so much in his theatre. On the seventeenth of February, Armande and Baron, seeing he was at the end of his strength, begged him not to play that evening: "What do you expect me to do?" he answered. "There are fifty poor workmen who have only their wages to live on; what will they do if I don't play? I should reproach myself for having neglected to give them bread a single day, if I could possibly do so . . ."

Aside from Tartuffe, Don Juan and Harpagon, which of the ridiculous heroes of Molière would not be capable, at least once, of attaining that charity? From what man could we not expect that proof of a lofty origin, an eminent vocation? Molière dying raises up the man that Molière the living had abased. He gave up his spirit, Ramon Fernandez tells us, in the arms of two nuns to whom he was giving hospitality: "He gave evidence to them of all the sentiments of a good Christian and all the resignation that he owed to the will of the Lord."

VOLTAIRE VERSUS PASCAL

A̲FTER BLAISE PASCAL'S DEATH, AND EVEN BEFORE THE manuscript of the *Pensées* was published, although his genius was beyond question, he still remained a party man in the eyes of many. Voltaire's eye was needed to discern in the great man of Port-Royal, in the enemy of the Molinists, the leader who would soon rally all the forces of French Catholicism. Voltaire, wishing to crush the "beast," saw very well what a lofty head would have to receive the first blow.

It was not at first because he hated Pascal, the Jansenist, the insulter of the Fathers to whom he owed his profound humanist studies. He remembered gratefully the College of Clermont and recognized his debt toward the Fathers Porée, Tournemine and Toulié. What he liked in the Jesuits was just what made them odious to Pascal, and he approved the fact that religion, thanks to them, was becoming more supple, less sure of itself. In *The Century of Louis XIV*, he claims to absolve them of everything of which Pascal accuses them: "It is true that the whole book is based on a false premise; it skillfully attributed to the whole Society extravagant opinions of several Spanish and Flemish Jesuits. They could have been dug up just as well from the Dominican and Franciscan casuists . . . But it was not a question of being right. Nothing was ever so hateful to Voltaire as the terrible Jansenist gentlemen of the robe in Parliament. It was a question of amusing the public . . ." Moreover, there, perhaps, he lost the scent. For what he calls "beast," that religion so hated, bore in it (at least in France) a deadly germ which was that same Jansenism; and from Voltaire's point of view, the best policy would have been, perhaps, not to combat it, but to let it destroy itself. Aside from the fact that there is doubtless a Jansenist heredity in certain forms of modernism, it could not be repeated too often that, had it triumphed, the doctrine of Port-Royal would have created a desert in the Church; for how can one live under the law of terror and despair! If our Pascal who dared to write: "Nothing can be understood if one does not accept as a principle that He wanted to blind some and enlighten others," and again: "There is enough clarity to enlighten the elect and enough darkness to humiliate them. There are enough obstacles to blind the damned and enough light to condemn and render them inexcusable . . ." If Pascal, just the same, wept with joy, it was because he had had, through the miracle of the holy Thorn and his night of Monday, November 23, 1654, the assurance of being eternally chosen, of being reprieved (this legal term could come from the word "grace" in the Jansenist sense). Yes, in order to destroy Christianity more effectively, Voltaire ought to have supported that frightful doctrine that prompted Monsieur de Saint-Cyran to congratulate himself so for the early death of his own niece: "It happens occasionally that a single person is saved in a large and numerous family, and the succession of the damned in the other world is sometimes, from father to son, as long as the duration of the family; this takes place almost always in the houses of the rich, and perhaps none will be saved, if they remain in the swim of the world, except those who die early." (Collection of several selections to be used for a history of Port-Royal, Utrecht, 1740).

But Voltaire's weakness for his former teachers and his aversion to Jansenists would not have been enough to unleash him against Pascal, if he had not foreseen the thousands of souls directed, brow-beaten in future centuries, by that passionate logic; if he had not understood that that huntsman in the service of the "beast" would hunt on the very terrain of the Encyclopedia, and that he would make scholars, artists and philosophers crash down at the foot of the cross of Christ.

Let us render him this justice that, aside from a few remarks ventured touching on the depths and folly of Pascal, Voltaire never tried to bring down so lofty an enemy. "For a long time I have wanted to fight that giant,"—he cried to Formont (June, 1733) —"No warrior is so well armed that one can not pierce a weak spot in his armor . . ." So this puny David, armed with the sling-stone of common sense, advances toward the Christian Goliath. He takes stock of him and admires him. At first a literary admiration; and if it is true that an author only admires himself in others, was there not already some of Voltaire in the zest of the *Provinciales?* The same Latin earth nourished those two indomitable spirits. In respect to the first of the "little letters," Arouet [1] pronounces the name of Molière, which is tantamount to recognizing himself a brother in common with Pascal. Besides, he grants his enemy "every kind of eloquence," and histories of literature have reproduced a hundred times Voltaire's judgment which dates the stabilization of the language from the *Provinciales.*

So he did not fail to recognize the genius to which he devoted his famous *Remarks* which are to be found joined to his *Philosophical Letters,* and of which Sainte-Beuve said, with some exaggeration, but with striking imagery: "that they get Pascal right under the hair-shirt." In order to measure Vol-

[1] Voltaire's family name. Transl. note.

taire's passion at that time, we must resort to his correspondence: "Get along, Pascal! Leave me alone!" he exclaims
in a letter to d'Argental (May 1734) .—"You have a chapter
on the prophets that does not have a shadow of common
sense. Hold on!" (It must be confessed that this Voltaire is
pretty likable.) In April, he wrote to Maupertuis: "Do you
know I did a remarkable favor for that Pascal? Of all the
prophecies he relates, there is not a one which can be applied
to Jesus Christ. His chapter on the miracles is meaningless
chatter. Yet I did not say anything, and they protest." Indeed Voltaire does not hide from Formont that he will have
the prudence not to touch on dangerous subjects in the
Pensées. "I shall take precautions. I shall criticize only the
places which are not so bound up with our holy religion that
one can not scratch Pascal's skin without making Christianity
bleed." (June 1733) .

But here prudence did him a service, since it made him
pass over those very frail passages of the Pascalian apologetics (prophecies) , to attach himself to the essential which
he himself just about summarizes in the two propositions: 1—
It is not enough, as Pascal would have it, for a religion to
take account of human nature to be true; 2—That twofold
human nature which Pascal imagines and which, according
to him, makes Christianity necessary, does not exist. At least
on the first of those propositions, a theologian would agree
with Voltaire who, moreover, explains himself in a letter to
his former teacher, Father Tournemine. The truth is that
Pascal did not support it under that absolute form either.
The conformity between human nature and Catholicism does
not prove the truth of that religion, nor that it is revealed,
but restrains the mind, and incites it to search further in
that direction, rather than in the other. As little interested
as we are in the argument that was drawn later from the

moral and social advantages of Christianity (for a mistake, however beneficent, is not worth the sacrifice of a moment of pleasure) , so much the more are we struck by the relationship of the key to its lock that Pascal was the first to show between our nature and Catholic doctrine. And one knows all the arguments that have been gotten from it in our day by such apologists as that astonishing Chesterton, whose famous passage must always be quoted: "When we find something strange in Christianity, it is, in the last analysis, because there is something strange in reality . . ."

But the most intriguing thing is to see the future author of *Candide*, he who was to administer such a fine horse-whipping to the optimists, shocked by the too dark picture of man that Pascal outlines for us, and denouncing that "lofty misanthrope." Against Pascal, Voltaire would be tempted to maintain that this world is the best of worlds! It is true that he is young at this time, and that it is the season of soft living. No one, in those frivolous years, thinks of taking anything tragically. Why despair because we do not know anything about the nature of our thoughts? As for the eternal silences of the infinite spaces, Voltaire does not doubt that progress in enlightenment will soon make it less fearful. He sees no contradiction in man, treats as "high fallutin" nonsense (for to-day that is the word of critics who do not understand a text) Pascal's thought touching the carnal order as opposed to the spiritual order, bypassed infinitely by that of charity. It was a French Protestant, established at Utrecht, Monsieur Boullier, who, with much power and good sense, refuted Voltaire's objections. Way down deep, they did not even shake the colossus. After Voltaire, Condorcet will add only a little trifle to Pascal's amulet, or to that "chasm on the right" of which it is a question only in one of the Abbé Boileau's letters, printed in 1737! Later it will be up to the opponent to persuade himself that, in the scientific century (as though Pascal's century was not a scientific one!) Pascal would have endorsed Free Thinking—he for whom faith escaped reason, and who had an entirely inner knowledge of God:

GOD PERCEPTIBLE TO THE HEART
NOT TO THE MIND

JEAN-JACQUES ROUSSEAU

I

The Confessions

IT IS NOT ENOUGH TO SAY THAT JEAN-JACQUES IS CLOSE TO us; he is one of us. His contemporaries and the generation that followed his have retained his redundancy and his eloquence. They have extracted from his general ideas all the absurd, and all the tragic, too. They have, in a manner of speaking, filtered Rousseau. And that part of his inheritance that comes down to us is his inner attitude—a certain irritated satisfaction in being himself. This master of falsehood and pride finds his true friends among us.

To-day whether Jean-Jacques arouses love or hatred, we love him as ourselves, and hate him as ourselves. The affection he awakens in us does not prevent us from seeing clearly. It is not what he confesses that makes us know him. We know him because we have one consciousness with him; we are his consciousness.

And in the same way, the dislike and aversion it is impossible not to feel for him is never unaccompanied by collusion. Even when he annoys us the most, we do not fail to discover in him that savor one finds only by oneself.

Nothing resembles us less than our own acts; that is what we learned from him in the first place. Rousseau treats his

defects as he treated his children: he does not recognize
them. And that is not all: he never doubted that he was the
father of his poor children, and he does doubt being the
author of certain frightful gestures. But if he is not their
author, it must then be the rest of the world. This step is soon
passed over.

Jean-Jacques is the best of men. Yet he accused the servant
Marion of a petty theft he himself had committed. He has
the most tender heart in a century that shed so many tears
before cutting off so many heads. But the most tender-hearted
of all men deserts his five children. He has the courage to
accomplish this atrocious act five times. He confesses it, for
he is sincere. Sincerity, the pleasure of public confession, we
have found in his descendants. It is true he bequeathed us, at
the same time, a method, so that confession should cost us
very little,—a method in two points, which attain such a degree of perfection with him that his sons of to-day have been
able to add nothing to it: it is first a question—and this is
the first "period"—of establishing the fact that in so far as
our acts deserve blame, society bears the burden of them.

Society, the scapegoat that assumes all Jean-Jacques'
offences, is not, in his eyes, an abstract power. When he writes
"society," he thinks "the others" and among the others, the
Great,—those who took such care of him, spoiled him, fed
his vanity, who entered with so much devotion into all his
likes and dislikes. And yet how he hates them! If he had been
a prophet, I doubt that the vision of the guillotine would
have wrenched from him much more than hypocritical tears.
"Why didn't I marry?" he wrote to Madame de Francueil,
who questioned him on the desertion of his five children. "In-
quire of your unjust laws, Madame . . . It is the estate of
the rich, it is your estate that steals from mine my children's
bread." It is the law's fault . . . But, in Jean-Jacques' eyes,

these laws are Madame de Francueil's. He has incarnated them in that woman and it is that woman whom he hates. Neither the favors of Madame de Warens, nor those of Madame d'Epinay and Madame d'Houdetot, nor the patient kindness shown him by the Marshal of Luxembourg, Milord Maréchal and so many other great lords, prevailed against that hatred preserved and cooked over again. Envy, that base passion for equality which is the mark of our era, already exists full grown in Rousseau. That the prerogatives of the Great could offend him, he denies with a fury that proves conclusively that those who accuse him of it, have touched the spot: "Philosophers," they say, "would like to confuse all the states and pay respect to no one. No, Sirs, no. Philosophers don't wish to confuse anything; they are not jealous of the good fare which is killing you, nor of the carriage that prevents you from using your legs, nor of the impudent servants who steal from you and make you hateful so often; they do not even refuse to render you your due; just as they would have made no objections, in ancient Greece, to paying reverence to the idols that had no meaning."

A little jar of butter, sent to Thérèse Levasseur, was left by mistake at the home of the Count de Lastic who thought it was his, and at first refused to give it back to Thérèse's mother. It could be observed to what point Jean-Jacques' insolence mounted on this occasion! "I tried to console the good woman in her affliction, by explaining to her the rules of high society and well-bred people; I proved to her that it would not be worth while having a retinue if it were not used to send away the poor man when he comes to claim what belongs to him; and, by showing her that justice and humanity are vulgar words, I finally made her understand that she was highly honored to have a count eat her butter."

A vengeful note on "the man with the butter" is to appear

in the *Nouvelle Héloise*. Heaven and earth must be moved
to allay the wrath of the great outraged citizen. Madame
d'Epinay gets down on her knees; Madame de Chenonceaux
entreats him: "A minute of misunderstanding, whose import
may have been very badly related to you, should not prevail
against the apologies and civilities that I myself have been
empowered to offer you in their behalf." Elsewhere the
great lady writes humbly to his Philosophical Majesty!
"Since I am engaged in asking your pardon . . ." How heavy
with significance is that petty incident! We understand that
gentlemen of the robe, who, moreover, washed their hands,
and had experience and education, enjoined Sanson to pay
society the civilities that they had showered upon their father
Jean-Jacques. In Rousseau, resentment became creative, but
of all his sons, it is perhaps Robespierre who is most like
him.

Yet no massacre will divert the aristocracy from coddling
the Jean-Jacques of all times. The "I hate you" that they pass
from mouth to mouth, and that the head of French socialism
was offering only yesterday, would not cost him a single in-
vitation if he had a notion to dine in town. In the first place,
because men of the world, in spite of all that is said, often
have a sincere worship of the mind, respect for talent and a
passion to serve it; and also because they are bored with each
other,—and above all because the true anarchists, anarchists
in their pure state, those whose revolt has its source neither
in poverty nor hatred, nor in envy, are more commonly found
in parlors than among the people. This strange liking of
society people for the kind of man who works to have their
heads cut off, may irritate, but it is not base, surely less base
than the hatred Jean-Jacques aroused in French society, fol-
lowing those June days, and which forced Sainte-Beuve to
handle the *Confessions* with gloves on under the pretext

"that there is not a writer more fitting to render the poor man superb."

So society assumes the short-comings of Jean-Jacques. That is what makes confession easy. But he wants to make it still easier. It is not enough to avoid all blame, the most subtle (and this is the second "period") is to obtain an increased reputation and to push audacity to the point of offering to God the ridiculous prayer of the Pharisee that serves as a prelude to the *Confessions*: "Eternal Being, gather about me the great crowd of my fellow-men, so they may listen to my confessions, so they may groan for my indignities and blush for my misery. May each one, in his turn, uncover his heart at the foot of Thy throne with the same sincerity; and may a single one say to You, if he dare: 'I was better than that man.' "

Poor Jean-Jacques! No offense that he confesses can cause as much horror as such a word. It is enough to drag him down lower than the most infamous of men, who has taken measure of his baseness, who has beaten on his breast before infinite Purity and tremblingly repeated Saint-Peter's prayer: "Depart from me, Lord, for I am a sinner."

It remains for Jean-Jacques to persuade those who would hesitate to absolve him of his offenses in order to heap them on society, that his faults are not faults. This is the miracle of the new Messiah, the Wedding in Cana where evil is changed into good. Until the time of the Geneva citizen, murderers and libertines did not set themselves up as examples, nor sodomites teach morals, and courtesans answered abuse by the admirable words of some royal mistress or other to a man who was insulting her: "Since you know who I am, Sir, do me the favor of praying to God for me." Jean-Jacques can take up the word of the *Médecin malgré lui*: "We have changed all that." The heart is on the right, the liver on the left. Rousseau committed an outrage much more serious than the simple reversal of the tribunal of the conscience which condemned all offenses,—yet an outrage for which, Bossuet assures us, there is almost no cure. Jean-Jacques did not destroy the conscience; he corrupted it. He adjusted it to lies and falsehood. And it is only after being assured it will henceforth render only oracles favorable to his passion that he installs this soiled conscience on the very throne of God, that he adores it, that he addresses prayers to it: "Conscience, divine instinct . . ."

Among a thousand examples, there is none more surprising than the famous letter to Madame de Francueil: "Yes, Madame, I put my children in a Foundling Asylum; I committed them to the charge of an institution made for that. If my poverty and misfortunes deprive me of the power of fulfilling so dear a duty, it is a misfortune for which I should be pitied and not a crime for which I should be blamed. I owe them a livelihood and I have procured a better and more sure one for them than I should have been able to give them myself (Could "tartuffery" be pushed further?) . . . To support my children and their mother with the blood of misery? (He meant: to support them with his literary work!) No, Madame, it is better for them to be orphans than to have a knave for a father!"

Jean-Jacques' whole work (especially his correspondence) would furnish us as many texts as we would want, like that one, in which it appears no man has, perhaps, carried the corruption of the inner senses so far. Virtue is now becoming the dummy for crime; now the conscience-divine-instinct is erected for the approval of mass murders whose time is approaching.

How far Rousseau is from Christianity, in spite of his professions of faith! I deny that, face to face with the atheism of the philosophers, he was even the soiled representative of Christianity. The presence of Grace in a man is measured by the clarity of the eye with which he judges. Salvation is not far away when we begin to see ourselves as we really are. Detestation of oneself increases with holiness, and the nearer a man draws to God, the more clearly the eternal light reveals his own blemishes. The complacency and satisfaction of a Rousseau in being oneself, is perhaps the feeling furthest away from the Christian. A few praises addressed to Christ can not balance it. When Jacques Maritain, in his admirable study on the *Three Reformers*, denounces in Rousseau a finished example of religious thought, anti-intellectual, pragmatist and immanentist, perhaps he pays him too high a compliment. For these various errors, especially the latter, are not always incompatible with a life of prayer, not even perhaps with a life of union, and all the self-denial such a life includes. There is not even enough Christianity in Rousseau to make a heretic of him.

It is not that some traces of Christian humility can not be found in him. Yes, indeed, when he writes to his friend Altuna: "I draw a favorable augury from the bitter trials that it has pleased God to send me. I have so greatly deserved punishment that I have no right to complain of them; and since He begins with justice, I hope He will finish with mercy . . ." You must know that this friend to whom he is writing is very pious and has reprimanded him . . . But there we do not recognize Rousseau's accent. That is not his true thought.

For he was never a Catholic. At Turin, the young Rousseau is led on to conversion by the basest of sentiments. He himself does not conceal the shame that this self-interested conversion caused him. But his sincerity does not go far enough to recognize that he avenges himself for this shame on Catholicism. A guilty conscience soils everything it approaches. Because Rousseau does not give his heart's assent to the Church, he insists she requires only blind submission. He imputes to her the baseness of his own feelings. And that is what renders him unpardonable, in spite of his youth and circumstances fitting to extenuate his fault.

But Rousseau always lied; and the modern era rests altogether on Rousseau's falsehood—that essential falsehood: the transmutation of base lead into pure gold, of evil into good. This reversal appears in a text like Madame de Francueil's letter with an ingenuity that provokes laughter. As long as Jean-Jacques makes use only of his mind to convince us, everyone, according to his temperament, becomes angry or amused; but no one any longer takes him seriously. If he had only been what they called a philosopher in the eighteenth century, he would have been one of the lowest order—although at that time one was a philosopher without much trouble. It is the artist in him that charms and that has poisoned the world. We laugh when, in a letter, he boasts of having abandoned his children—but we weep with tenderness over the idyl of Charmettes. That is because in it he does not try to convince us; he listens to his heart, becomes intoxicated with his memories, is charmed with himself. In vain we are warned of the fraud: it spreads out all over, and never was the Infinite Being, Virtue, mingled with a more disturbing or uglier story. We know it and we know under what fine pretexts Madame de Warens covers up the favors she diverts —partly only—from the domestic, Claude Anet, and that she pours out on the pretty neophyte. It is a question of saving him from worse; it is a question of doing him good. All the Warenses of to-day have brought to perfection this method of "doing good": "I could not desert him," they say, "I'll raise him up; I'll educate him; I'll marry him off." (And so Mad-

ame de Warens makes the proposal herself when the young
Wintzenreid, the boy who succeeded Rousseau in her favor,
decides to marry.)

Is not this disturbing maternity her most secret pleasure?
But what now:

> *Calm sanctuaries! Calm years! Calm retreats!*
> *Rustling young alders sang among the beeches.*
> *One sometimes received the visit of a priest . . .*

Those auxiliary love affairs, that sharing, all that should
fill one with horror, and nothing shocks. We are accomplices
in spite of ourselves. The magician invests the most corrupt
customs with all the graces of purity.

It is to this hypochondriac, to this victim of persecution,
that humanity perhaps owes the picture of the most enchant-
ing happiness. This sick lover, whose sentimental life knew so
few victories, leaves us this eternally fresh picture of his first
love. At Charmettes, he seems to say to us, we were not guilty
because we were ourselves. We took care not to be high-
falutin'. We did not permit any touching up of God's work
within us. And it is true that Madame de Warens never
thought that her religion could interfere with her pleasures in
any way. "One must be oneself," Rousseau repeated. "One
must remain oneself." To-day that is the device of all his
children. We tell ourselves in vain that what genius makes so
attractive, is just the same, beastly. But there are the bowers,
the terraced garden between the vine and the orchard, the
little chestnut wood, the fountain . . . Unrestrained, the
wind stirs the trees; the sun shines down on the roofs and
makes the china on the set table glisten. Mythological shepherds and fabulous animals no longer stand between us and
reality. Human history is rooted, framed and related in objects, odors and instants.

"Here begins the short happiness of my life . . ." Did he suspect that there was beginning, too, the intoxication of a world? But one had to wait a century and a half for the poison to accomplish its work: only to-day do we see its final effects. All of romanticism, literally faithful to Jean-Jacques, continued to believe in virtue. It cost it little more than it cost the Geneva citizen, to love it without practicing it, and to adore that outer divinity, inaccessible to the heart of poor men. But to-day, virtue after the pattern of Rousseau resides deep within our flesh; it has become our very flesh, its basest passion, its strangest and most unhappy inclination. That is still saying too much; it is interwoven with our own changing. In his day, Rousseau abstained from putting any order into his *Reveries,* because, said he, "order would divert me from my aim, which is to remark the modifications in my soul and their succession . . ." There is a sentence that gives out a modern note, if I may say so.

And yet! Shall we join Rousseau's enemies to accuse him of every iniquity? Let us be afraid of giving in to the inclination to discover the source of our misery, cost what it may, and to give it a name. Rousseau's work, before being the cause of so many regrettable effects, is itself a result. Rousseau may be the father of the modern world, but first of all, it is the modern world that secreted Rousseau. A prolonged constraint has been set free in him. Like Luther, he is the outcropping, or the spurting up of accumulated subterranean forces. Deliverance, liberation which made him weak with joy on the road to Vincennes. He who maintained that the progress of the arts and sciences had corrupted customs, did not accuse artists and writers of that crime: "It was," he wrote to Voltaire, "neither Terence, nor Cicero, nor Virgil, nor Tacitus, it was not scholars or poets who caused the misfortunes of Rome or the crimes of the Romans; but without the slow, secret poison that, little by little, corrupted the most vigorous government history has ever mentioned, neither Cicero, nor Lucretius, nor Sallust would have existed or written." Here Rousseau presents his own defense, for he himself was the outlet through which all the pus of a decayed organism was escaping. But let us render him this justice. What comes out of him is not only all the disturbance of an era; he had the clearest vision of the problems of every order that were being presented at that time. Should we impute guilt to him for having proposed solutions with too much eloquence and the most dangerous passion?

We are sometimes inclined to see in him less a victim than a dangerous and irritating fool. It is true that if Rousseau charmed his century, he was, at the same time, unbearable to it. To-day there is no longer any society in the sense in which one then understood it. How would the salons of Paris have tolerated that insolent plebeian? High society indeed consented to opening the windows and looking at the green, but not to giving up the pleasure of being witty and of talking. Rousseau's greatest offence was his passion for solitude. By sensitive souls, which, in another connection, recognized themselves in him, he was reviled on account of that peculiarity. The most sagacious already foresaw that this embittered plebeian was a dangerous man, and the philosophers were irritated that sentiment should be given precedence over reason. They refused to go down on all fours and browse.

During his lifetime, he had enough enemies at his heels to have the right to cry out against persecution without anyone crying out: "Crazy man!" To tell the truth, his folly is not because he was convinced he was persecuted—which is true—but in thinking everyone was entirely taken up with Jean-Jacques. Such is the exaggeration of his ego: he does not doubt that a single combat exists between Jean-Jacques and the rest of the world. "He thinks," he writes of himself, in the second dialogue, "that all the disasters of his destiny, since his unfortunate fame, are the fruits of a far-reaching and secret plot, formed by a few persons who have found the way to make everyone whom they need for its execution join: the Great, the authors, the doctors, all the men of influence, all the women of the town, all accredited bodies," etc., etc.

What is true is that he had the misfortune to displease, at the same time, both the pious and the Encyclopedists: irreconcilable enemies who became reconciled on his back. And to-day still he has against him—in addition to the pious— philosophers and humanists. Just as the Encyclopedists despised him because instead of judging him by his desires, good will and the impulses of his heart, they judged him by his actions, so to-day he looks like a liar because *The Confessions, The Reveries* and *The Dialogues* show us a man who, not recognizing his acts, believes he is virtuous when he aspires to be so. Such is the eternal misunderstanding between Rousseau and the rest of the world.

His opponents, philosophers and humanists, have the right, in the name of logic, to reproach him with the contradiction between what he claims to be and what he is. But if he had claimed only to follow his passions, if he had not played the virtuous man, by what categorical moral could they have condemned him? Let us recognize it: Certain of Rousseau's faults, by any standard, cause horror. I am thinking especially of the ribbon theft of which he accused the servant Marion, and the desertion of his five children. For this last offence, one would be tempted to go further than Rousseau himself: that action resembles him so little that one yields to the desire to believe that he did not commit it. What is incredible is not that he took one new-born babe to the orphanage; what surpasses all belief is that he repeated the offence five times, that he had the persevering courage; and that he did not even feel sufficient aversion for it to keep himself from giving life in the future. Now this is striking: when he returned to Geneva in 1754, followed by Thérèse, and decided to go back to the Protestant Church, several members of the Consistory wanted to keep him from Communion because he was living with a woman out of wedlock, and because she slept in his room. Here is Rousseau's defense: "If my situation were known to those people, they would be convinced that I am absolutely incapable of carrying out their suspicions. For a long time, I have suffered terrible pains from an incurable retention of urine, caused by an excrescence in the urethra, that stops up that canal to such an extent that even Daran's bougies have never been able to enter."

This text makes clear that Rousseau's infirmity had deprived him for a long time of all sexual intercourse. Now there is no offense of which an impotent man would not accuse himself in order to hide his misfortune. In Stendhal's *Armance*, the impotent Octave goes to the point of pretending to his mistress that in his childhood he had a passion for stealing. He speaks to her continuously of fatal peculiarities; he sends her astray with a thousand clews, makes himself appear, in her eyes, as a debauched man. Let her think him capable of everything, but above all, let her not know he is incapable of possessing her!

That invention of Rousseau's seems to us similar. How fearful the mockery of a Diderot or a Grimm could appear to him! If he had had normal relations with Thérèse, would he, as he did, have taken the whole family Levasseur on his

back? It seems as though this woman, almost an idiot, had
the right to demand everything and that she expected com-
pensations from him. Can't we imagine Rousseau letting himself go, by vanity and false shame, into this invention without understanding at first what a terrible load he was assum-
ing before a world that did not yet know him? Some day,
when he has become very famous, he will awaken prisoner
of his lie—too late to deny it, even to himself. Yes, all that
would be credible, and even likely, if specialists did not in-
sist they had found traces of the little abandoned children.
Jules Lemaître who at first defended, with great ingenuity,
the thesis of the invention and the lie, lays down his arms before proofs which, it seems to me, are not conclusive. The
supposition remains that the children were not "his"; that
Thérèse (who is suspected of not having waited for Jean-
Jacques' death in order to take a pretty lowly lover) had
yielded, as others have done, to the demands of a holy
nature . . .

But let us leave that. After all the offences he confesses,
that man remains, none the less, in Voltaire's century, God's
wretched defender. At a time when the poverty-stricken
thought of Voltaire passed for philosophy, it was fitting that
the supernatural be defended by that maniac, that madman.
If we look for Bossuet's descendant in the eighteenth century,
we find no other than the solitary wanderer. There, indeed,
was the age of the great Catholic humiliation! It is not sufficient to say that sometimes Jean-Jacques rediscovers Bossuet's eloquence; what is most astonishing is that he refound
also his indomitable good sense and clear thinking. Especially
in private letters in which he tries to appease the priests, a
prey to doubt, or anxious young Catholics, one is amazed to
find, under his pen, the expression of an almost earthy wis-

dom, advice practical and void of all pathos and lofty pad-
ding.

Lastly, let us do him this justice: however far he may be
from true Christianity, he confessed Christ before men, and
that too will be counted for him. Apart from the comparison
between the death of Christ and that of Socrates, he said of
Jesus' gentleness "that it was more angelic and divine than
human"; and that the Gospels could not be read without
weeping. The Vicar of Savoy does not blaspheme against the
sacrifice of the Mass: "Whatever might be said of this inconceivable mystery, I do not think that, on the day of the Last
Judgment, I shall be punished for ever having profaned it in
my heart."

Doubtless, this profession of faith should have been enough
to win him the right to attain the light, if he had not been
to such a degree a prey to himself. When he fancies he is
leaving the world, it is only that his immoderate personality
does not distinguish the world any more; it scarcely dis-
tinguishes God. And that is why the apologists should use it
only with prudence. To help us measure the poverty of
Rousseau's Christianity, Jacques Maritain alludes to another
solitary wanderer of the eighteenth century, Benoît-Joseph
Labre, under his rags and vermin, whose feet bled on the
roads of France and Italy at that time. Without a doubt, a
certain Catholic revival in the nineteenth century had its
source in Jean-Jacques, and text books have the right to teach
us that Chateaubriand was born of him. But it is a question
of knowing what the *Génie du Christianisme* is worth, *sub
specie aeterni;* and if that apology conceived in Madame de
Beaumont's bedroom is of a higher order than the effusions
of the catechumen of Charmettes and his pious mamma, lifted
up to the Author of nature. We owe the religious awakening
of the nineteenth century in part to Rousseau, it is true, but

the essence of Catholic life does not abide in the troubled stream of which he is the source—the mire.

The eye is struck by a shallow which runs from Madame Guyon to Madame de Warens, from Rousseau to Chateaubriand and to Lamennais. But the true current, the one with great depths, springs up under the hazeltrees of Paray-le-Monial at the decline of a great century, flows unseen or scorned, under the feet of Benoît Labre (whose pilgrimage begins just at Paray); comes to light at Ars in the vicarage of a lost village. Alone, the most humble and ignorant dowsers uncover for the eyes of the world this water hidden deep down in the earth. The shepherds of La Salette pick up a secret; and between the rock and the mountain torrent, that calm little girl with a somewhat backward mind and an ordinary face, Bernadette Soubirous, forgets to pick up her wood and falls on her knees. Lastly, the demon of boredom and lucre unleashed against the little sister Thérèse does not succeed in darkening that martyred childish face.

Sometimes the deep inner river and the shallow current of Rousseau seem to draw near to each other and mingle their streams: in Lamennais and Lacordaire. But one stream always has to divert the other. Rousseau triumphs in Lamennais. By dint of humility and love, Lacordaire dominates the Geneva demon of eloquence without ever completely conquering him.

On the religious plane, Jean-Jacques Rousseau seems to us to have no other reason for existing than to offer the world a caricature of Catholicism. He is a kind of "skinned" Christian at the service of Nietzsche. Here is the privileged subject in whom break out all the defects of the slave. Here you have the weakest of the weak, the infirm, the madman interested in the great Christian treason, in the reversal of all values! How insignificant the services that Rousseau could render Christ, at the price of arms with which he enriches the opponents of the Cross, seem to us! Not that he wanted it that way; it is without knowing it that he deprives Christianity of its essence: to die in order to be born again; to die to oneself so as to be reborn in Christ, that is the secret that Jean-Jacques Rousseau either did not know or scorned. Only he finds it pleasing to think himself immortal. So he retains from religion a hope of survival. He can not give up the perspective of finding himself again after death. Why refuse oneself this consolation? It costs so little to pretend to believe it: "Illusion, perhaps," he dares to write; "but if I knew a more consoling one, I would adopt it . . ."

There you have the cowardly, fearful being whom Nietzsche denounces: "The one who thinks only of strict usefulness." Perhaps Nietzsche was not thinking of Rousseau when he wrote that; but when he added: "One scorns the suspicious being, with his restless glance, the one who abases himself, the man-dog who lets himself be ill-treated, the servile flatterer and above all the liar . . ." That involuntary portrait seems to us more shrieking of likeness than la Tour's pastel.

There is no denying that a work must be very alive still for us to keep on protesting against it after a century and a half —and with what heat! Our forefather Jean-Jacques is younger than his son Chateaubriand and his grandsons, the Romantics. They sleep, embalmed in their glory. He is one of us: I close with this word with which I began—his name is Romain Rolland, Marcel Proust, André Gide. Entire pages of the *Confessions* or the *Reveries* could be inserted into *Swann's Way* without it being easy to detect the fraud. May my shocked readers pardon me for thinking that such vehemence, in which love and hatred are mingled, is exactly what every dead writer would most desire to inspire, if he were still alive.

II

The Solitary Wanderer

A T A TIME WHEN SOCIETY LIFE WAS ATTAINING PERFECTION, Jean-Jacques came to preach solitude and shocked everyone. By proclaiming, contrary to Rousseau, that only the evil stay alone, Diderot expressed the opinion of right-thinking people, much more hostile to solitude than they had been under the deceased King. In the seventeenth century it was admitted that a soul in love with God might retire from the world. The Court and the City were entirely willing that a right-thinking man, worn out with riotous living and wearied by intrigues, should retreat and take account of his soul. The Misanthrope would not have seemed at all ridiculous if the "place of retirement" whose refuge he desired had been located in the Chevreuse Valley: at Port Royal. But Alceste claimed to retire from the world only to be free to be an honest man and because of disappointed love, and that is why he lends himself to laughter.

But in the philosophical century, the loftiest excuse for solitude, God, no longer existed in the eyes of the intelligentsia. So what fly had bitten that Genevan so that he wanted to destroy, among honest men, sociability, the only pleasure after love (but they can not be separated) which helps us tolerate life, and diverts us from the thought of death? Moreover, the preaching of Rousseau was that of the fox with his tail cut off. He admits, in many a passage of the *Confessions*, to the timidity of an inferior, adding that he had never been more than half-witted.

He did not shine in the world and only succeeded moderately with his quips, affectations and peculiarities. At every moment, one feels he is ready to invent the expression "put your foot into it," so exactly does this slang express his daily blunders. Like everyone of his kind, he thought he could get along by imitating the peasant of the Danube.

Madame d'Epinay called him her bear. But one soon tires of having a bear in the house. Rousseau was never a success. He made them laugh and got angry. The only course open to those who loved him, which was indeed to treat him as a genial animal whom one must defend against himself, hurt the substrata of plebeian and savage vanity in him. La Fontaine never felt humiliated at figuring in the menagerie of a great lady. But no one is less good-humored than this Rousseau who, at the height of his reputation, retains the sensitiveness, the suspicions and the insolence of subordinates. Sometimes it seems as though, if he accepts a hermitage, it is because he does not feel at ease at the table, and yet he can not sup in the pantry. Lastly, it is not at all certain that the citizen would have had Alceste's liking for retired spots if he had not suffered from the retention of urine which is, of all the diseases, the one that is the least consistent with the duties of the world.

But there are less base motives for Rousseau's bad-humor. This one especially must be considered: Rousseau, who did not acknowledge his children, did not acknowledge his acts either. He refused to establish any relationship between his love of virtue and the meanness of his life. His folly is born of this contrast; he wore himself out in the desire to resolve such a contradiction. Since he could not do it, he had no other resource than to burn his bridges, leave the world, act as little as possible, reduce to zero that social being whose every act was bad, and to have no more existence than an imaginary one in which his taste for virtue could be given free rein.

Without having passed the word along, it is certain all his

friends and enemies nudged him along that way. But if Rousseau did not acknowledge his acts, it was nevertheless according to them that the world judged him. And he who saw himself and knew his inner being and admired the soul within him, more in love with virtue than anyone else who ever existed, became vexed and indignant at the judgment men dared to pronounce upon him.

Legitimate irritation, to a certain extent. It is all too true that our acts do not always resemble us, and that is why any judgment pronounced on another is rash. But the ordinary mortal resigns himself to that rashness; not so Rousseau, who protested against the judgment of his century, and called upon future ages. It is for us that he wrote his *Confessions*, and above all his extraordinary *Dialogues*. But he comes to lose even this hope of being absolved by posterity. In which he was not mistaken much; Nietzsche's century, that of neo-classicism and neo-Thomism was to be harder on him than his contemporaries ever were. Voltaire, who hated him for hating art and in particular the theatre and for wanting us to get down on our hands and knees, did not know what we know to-day: that the end of the idyl would be terribly bloody.

So Rousseau lost faith even in future revenge. And as happens with certain souls, it was in total despair that he obtained peace. When he could expect nothing more from men, either from the living or from those who would come after him, his suspicions were ended. In the post-war Marcel Proust, we knew that state of mind, in which, behind universally benevolent formulas, is concealed a total detachment from everything human.

Such is Rousseau when he begins to write *The Reveries of a Solitary Wanderer*. This great imaginer who had tormented himself for such a long time by foreseeing what might threaten him, no longer feels himself threatened by anything: "Everything on earth is ended for me; one can no longer do me either good or harm; nothing remains for me to hope or fear in this world."

He is at the bottom of the pit; alone, and from now on insensitive, not with God, but "like God himself," he dares to write.

If he were with God, he would not add:

"In this world, I no longer have neighbor, nor comrade, no brother." (And here one thinks in spite of himself of that other solitary writer, Pascal: "I keep faith with all the world; I do not return evil to those who do it to me, but I wish for them a condition like mine in which one receives neither evil nor good from men. I try to be just, trustworthy, sincere and faithful to all men . . .")

There is no God less inward than Rousseau's Supreme Being. The Citizen never renounced the demands of the world to shoulder the infinite demands of Pascal's God. He no longer wishes anything but to remain alone with himself—which is not saying much, for to be is to act; and we know that at this time of his life, Rousseau claims to act as little as possible; since all his acts belie him, he sees no other remedy than not to move. "From now on, I am nothing among men, and that is all I can be, since I have no real connection with them any more, no more real commerce. Since I no longer can do any good that does not turn out badly, since I can no longer act without harming someone else or myself, my sole duty has become to abstain."

Perhaps he had the vague premonition that in the society from which he was separating himself forever, his works have introduced ferments that, at some later day, will avenge him for all he has suffered. An insect, after having laid her eggs, disappears. They will hatch out after Rousseau is no longer there. Rousseau, poor, sick, absurd, laughed at, incapable of changing himself, did not think himself powerless to transform society. He readily made Constitutions on order, for the use of Poland or Corsica. He thought he had recipes for making men happy; but he believed in them much less himself than the Jacobins were to do.

All of Rousseau's dreams which will soon be incarnated, which will become flesh and blood—especially blood—for the moment, help him to live. That is all he has in the world: no longer social and humanitarian dreams, but vague, soft impressions that are born in direct contact with nature. It is true that in the *Reveries*, he succeeds in giving us a direct sensation from that contact. For instance, when, in the course of the second Promenade, he is knocked down by a dog and faints: "Night was advancing," he wrote. "I saw the sky, some stars and a little green . . ." But everywhere in the fifth Reverie, which is an admirable symphony, we attend the indissoluble wedding of Rousseau with nature. His followers lost the secret of such a union. Nothing is further from the Rousseau of the fifth Reverie than romantic pride calling upon Cybele and asking her to render account of herself. The Romantic considers nature as a living being, he opposes her and treats her as one power against another. He descends to reproaches:

Nature with your calm face, how you forget! . . .

and with Vigny, one comes to insults:

You will not receive one cry of love from me.

Maurice de Guérin, much less demanding and much closer to Jean-Jacques, nevertheless deifies the inanimate world and penetrates it with the divine. The universe comes to life with his own passions, takes over his incurable sadness. How much closer Jean-Jacques is to us on the Island of Saint-Pierre than all the Romantic generation! No determination to deify: nature accompanies his dream, weds its meandering, supports it, directs it, gives it its form; as the banks do to the river, and they are not the river. It is because he brings to full fruition this balance, this harmony between the wanderer and the country he crosses that Rousseau, that man, persecuted and hypochondriac, has left us, perhaps, in his *Confessions* and in the fifth Reverie the most vivid pictures of human happiness. That adaptable mind, all made up of abandon and change, models effortlessly its impressions on the living matter: "I went to throw myself alone into a boat that I conducted to the middle of the lake when the water was calm, and there stretching out full length in the boat with my eyes turned toward the sky, I let myself float back and forth slowly for several hours, deep in a thousand dreams confused but delightful, which without having any other determined or constant object, did not fail to be a hundred times more to my taste than everything agreeable I have found in what one calls the pleasures of life . . ."

What Rousseau asks of nature is not to express his own passions or to reflect them; nor, emerging from his impassibility, to commiserate with him; nor to be moved because she endures while he is passing. No, he asks that she, by the trembling of the waters in the shadow, by the silent coming of night, by her freshness and perfumes, make him "feel his existence pleasurably without taking the trouble of thinking."

For, of all the reasons that detach Rousseau from the world and hand him over to nature, there is one more powerful than the others, it is laziness, his deep liking for inaction, for immobility and for emptiness. He is only fully satisfied in uncontrolled abandon to his dreams. Perhaps he hated men so much only because they interrupted his reverie. In his works such as *The Social Contract* and *Émile,* Jean-Jacques unburdens all at the same time whatever reasoning he bears within him; he frees himself of his systems, to which he himself attaches no practical value. But he is content only in that torpor favored by the earth, the water, the verdure, the light and the shadow; he likes only the enchantment of being in the world, simply, of seeing, breathing, touching, feeling, receiving all that opens up at the surface of consciousness and passes out when scarcely born.

At the end of his life, Rousseau retires more and more from Christian paths, and orients himself rather toward Buddhistic wisdom. He does not search for Life; nor exactly for the non-desire or the non-feeling; but he takes his stand between the two; he seems much nearer India than the Occident. That does not prevent Rousseau, especially the Rousseau of the *Reveries,* from keeping away from both of the two wisdoms, because he can not emerge from himself, escape from himself, neither as the Gospels wish it, nor as Hindu wisdom wants it. Incapable of losing himself to save himself, according to Christ, he is also incapable of losing himself in order to lose himself and destroy himself.

In the sixth Promenade, he says he is powerless to dislike anyone at all because: "I like myself too much," he says. "That would be restricting, limiting my existence, and I would rather stretch it out over the whole universe."

By that simple word, he relinquishes to us the key to his whole destiny. Rousseau swells up immoderately until he covers the world. He thinks he has deserted it, because he is equal to it. The solitary Wanderer has not fled the world, as he imagines, but the monstrous importance that he attributes to himself does not leave room for anyone near him. His solitude is only one aspect of his pride; and because at the time of the *Reveries*, that solitude seems absolute, we can conclude that his pride was one of the most absurd that have ever thrown a human brain into confusion.

For the solitary Wanderer to have brought to a good conclusion that fearful experience that tempted him, it would have been necessary for him, at the same time that he renounced the world of humans, to renounce that of color and form, and then finally himself, and that he consent to lose himself only to find himself again in the Infinite Being. But that is love, and the sensitive Jean-Jacques, who has spoken so much of love, never knew it, or knew only its shadow.

The Island of Saint-Pierre, in the middle of the Lake of Bienne, where the fifth Promenade takes us, separates him less from the world than he thinks. He has no need of an island, since he carries his prison everywhere with him. Not even a prison: a tomb. The ambulatory of his own heart in which he turns around is never walled. That Jean-Jacques, wandering about the faubourgs of Paris or on an enchanted island, remains inaccessible to both ill-will and charity. No longer can he have an interlocutor: neither alongside him, nor below him, nor above him. His ego fills up the entire capacity of his being. At the time of the *Reveries*, he no longer cares to escape; he doesn't try. In Rousseau's monstrous resignation to knowing nothing about himself, we must see a case of hypertrophy of the ego, but a very limited ego: tastes, appetites, manias and phobias. For there is a cell in the consciousness of oneself in which men and women have learned to surpass themselves. Jean-Jacques, himself, is like a lost person in the depths of his sensibility; he is submerged in it; and leagues of that ocean, dark and inhabited by monsters, separate him from mankind. At no time do we see him living in the center of himself. He never knew that upper part of the soul that Ruysbroeck compares to an eternal and living mirror of God. That ignorance was his illness; it was his folly, the folly of an imprisoned man who gropes for an escape and stumbles against invisible walls. He talks to himself, he gesticulates; and those who observe him from the outside interpret his gestures and words in their own way, deforming them and turning them against their author. His tender sensibility carries him toward them but, far from receiving him, they are suspicious and treat him as a sick man, as a dangerous nerve patient, and try to get rid of him. Poor Rousseau, consumed by a love that mankind does not want and to which he persists in offering no other object than himself! At no time does he suspect what such a demand means. The call of his soul remains without an echo from the direction of creatures and he does not think of the Creator. Or if he turns toward Him, it is generally only with a discourse of pompous verbalism. Never is he so eloquent as when he prays. Sometimes, doubtless, we feel him sincerely touched, but he is immediately satisfied with that emotion; he congratulates himself for it, he admires himself for it. Saint John of the Cross said that a monk who sees himself pray is not praying. Jean-Jacques never loses sight of himself, and it is when he should try to forget himself, to destroy himself, that his attention is redoubled.

On this point, the solitary Wanderer has not changed; he has remained just as he was when he was called the "Vicar of Savoy." The good vicar "converses" with God: he thinks that to pray to Him would be going contrary to the established order of wisdom. Jean-Jacques does not know what Christian prayer is and does not even suspect it: "I did all I could to reach the truth," said the Vicar of Savoy. But his source is too high up: when I have no more strength to go further, of what can I be guilty? It is for it to come to me . . ."

So he thinks that prayer (which he conceives only under its least purified form) is an insult to God; and a few lines further, he summons God to come to him. *Et Verbum caro factum est* . . . The Vicar of Savoy pronounces these words each morning and is never filled with their meaning. Nor Rousseau either, although a Christian. Yet he went from Protestantism to Catholicism, then returned to the Reformation. His mind must have been concerned with those problems for a long time, but always within himself, always absorbed, blinded by his ego. It is curious to see what the sky is for the Vicar of Savoy, and therefore also for the solitary Wanderer: "I aspire to the time when, freed of my bodily shackles, I shall be myself without contradiction, without sharing, and when I shall need only myself to be happy." All the profound and monstrous misery of Jean-Jacques is expressed in these words which are taken up by other hermits that the world taxes with folly, too: "In the evening of this life," said Saint John of the Cross, "you will be judged by your love." And again: "Lastly, we were only created for that Love . . . God is of no other use except that of love."

Jean-Jacques aspires to the time when he will need only himself to be happy. Yet it is to the extent that he can not get away from himself that he suffers, and there is the whole drama. The *Reveries* paint for us the time in his life when he thought he had attained a peace which was almost happiness, just because he had the illusion, thanks to nature, that he had left himself behind. The country where he botanizes frees Jean-Jacques from Jean-Jacques, at least he thinks so or wishes to persuade us it is so: "My imagination, which ignores painful objects," he wrote in his seventh Promenade, "allowed my senses to abandon themselves to the impressions light, but agreeable, of surrounding objects. My eyes travelled from one to the other without stopping, and it was impossible, in such a great variety, not to find something that would hold them more and stop them longer."

But doubtless a more difficult exercise than botany is necessary to obtain the dissolution of one's being in nature. To tell the truth, all the while that he was botanizing, the solitary Wanderer scarcely stopped ruminating over his troubles, turning and returning his inner field, and he always comes back to the old obsessions of his life. His walks in the country are in reality only walks through the past; and his feet always bring him back to the same circumstances which have never stopped tormenting him. In the ninth Promenade, there is scarcely anything but his love for children, although he has abandoned his; and in the tenth, there is only Madame de Warens; and in all of them, his enemies and persecutors. He congratulates himself on having left men, but those who were interwoven with his life, are carried everywhere with him.

The Solitary Wanderer is less solitary than he thinks; invisible, Grimm and Diderot remain the haunting companions of the way. He hears the children running around him breathless. He thinks he recognizes little faces shining with health and life raised toward him, the faces of those whom he has not recognized, both boys and girls. And in order to forget the girls, he recalls to himself in the same *Promenade,* the distribution of wafers which he made at a boarding-school on the grass of the Muette; and, in order to forget the boys, he gets sentimental over his kind heart on remembering the twelve measly apples that he divided among the little boys in Savoy during the fair of Chevrette: "I then had one of the most touching spectacles that can flatter a man's heart, that of seeing joy united to the innocence of that age breaking out all around me. For, on seeing it, even the spectators partook of it, and I, who shared this joy so cheaply, had also that of feeling it was my work."

Tartuffe distributed his pennies to the poor to be seen of Orgon. Rousseau showers unknown children with wafers and apples for the eyes of posterity, but posterity imagines that Rousseau's five children were not there to profit by such generosity. Poor old botanist! Just as there is false agaric, so there is false kindness, and Rousseau's herbarium is overflowing with it.

With false wisdom, too. This old man pretends to have found peace; but his walks are haunted by the phantoms of his enemies, his victims and his accomplices. He has forgotten nothing, nor has he learned anything. Nevertheless, the last interrupted sentence of the ninth Promenade lets us understand that he was beginning to feel how dishonorable his position in respect to Madame de Warens had been: "I was determined to use my leisure time to make it possible for me some day, if I could, to bring help to the best of women from whom I had received it."

In a less agreeable way than his five children, Jean-Jacques had been, himself, a child on charity; and all his life, he kept a liking for being supported. He never stopped being lodged by one of those great lords whom he treated in such a high-handed manner. His misanthropy did not go so far as to keep him from living at the expense of someone; not that he was miserly or self-seeking; but because he was incapable of making his way alone. He lived and died, not among friends, but among benefactors of the highest rank, and among charitable ladies of whom the first only, it is true, received in exchange what Jean-Jacques calls "his affectionate care."

Besides, he loved Madame de Warens, and he was still almost a child; we understand how at first he felt no embarrassment because of it. But when he is nothing more than an old man, given over entirely to morose delight, it appears that a wave of shame surges up and remains, like a fog, over the marshes left behind.

In his old age, Jean-Jacques wrongly boasts of knowing true peace at last. He is fooling himself, and he is fooling us if he wants to persuade us that he has made some progress toward virtue. Several of his biographers admit it; and Jules Lemaître insists strongly on the interrupted perfectioning of the poor man. To tell the truth, *The Reveries of a Solitary Wanderer* give evidence, at every moment, of his inclination to blame others for his own faults and to judge himself not by his frightful acts, but by his always lofty intentions. The principal theme of his famous and abominable letter to Madame de Francueil (in which he succeeds in finding a striking proof of his virtue in the desertion of his children) is shamelessly taken up again in the ninth Promenade: "I understand that the reproach for having put my children into a Foundling Asylum has easily degenerated, with a little twisting, into that of being an unnatural father and disliking the children. However, it is certain it was the fear of a destiny for them a thousand times worse, and almost inevitable by a very different way, that influenced me most in this step. Had I been more indifferent as to what would become of them, being in no condition to raise them myself, it would have been necessary in the state in which I am, to have let them be raised by their mother who would have spoiled them, or by her family, who would have made monsters of them. I still tremble at thinking of it . . . I knew that the least dangerous bringing up for them would be in the Home; and I put them there. I would do it again, with less hesitation too, if the thing were to be done over; and I know very well that no father is more tender-hearted than I would have been toward them; however little habit would have aided nature."

This text is enough to show how Rousseau remained the

same sinner who changes sin into virtue. He is still the same
sick man, and that is what excuses him. The solitary Wanderer still thinks he has the whole world at his heels. He
comes back to it ceaselessly in his *Reveries,* and does not mark
any progress on that level either. Nothing so monotonous as
folly. The resifting of a fixed idea gives off an unconquerable
boredom which has always kept us ourselves from feeling the
powerful charm of Jean-Jacques. But his sickness should keep
us even more from getting irritated or indignant. If his admirable *Reveries* do not reconcile us to the man, they increase
our pity for that great invalid. His sickness is above all
spiritual: strange obsidional delirium. He is a besieged man;
the entire world presses around him; he remains enclosed in
the most troubled region of himself and the most confused.
He knows vaguely that this could be his happiness and that
the kingdom of God is within him. At the same time, he feels
himself in a hurry to escape from himself, to lose himself to
find himself again, and he does not succeed in reconciling
those desires contradictory in appearance. That is because
this claimed Christian has never possessed the secret of
Christianity. He never entered into the mystery of Jesus.

It is fortunate for his memory that *The Reveries of a Solitary Wanderer* have given to us such a familiar and charming
picture of him which the future has retained in preference
to all the others. There he is as we love him: gentle old
botanist who is botanizing, as he copied music for a long time,
because a humble and regulated task appeases him, turns him
from his black thoughts. Was he so unhappy? What delight
for a Solitary Wanderer to feel upon him the attention of
Europe as he walks! How glad he is to bear the persecution
when he is assured of being the idol of his century! And is it
not a rare pleasure for that old botanist who botanizes to
think that posterity will see him eternally thus: on his knees
in the grass before a flower?

CHATEAUBRIAND

THIS FRANÇOIS DE CHATEAUBRIAND, SHORT OF STATURE, too broad shouldered, with his fine eyes, his hair always standing on end, his train of "ladies" (as Madame de Chateaubriand called her husband's mistresses), is perhaps the only writer, along with Goethe, who has imposed upon posterity the exact picture he resolved to leave to it. There he is, on his minstrel-style pedestal, that model and despair of all those like Barrès, who have come from him, not "such as eternity finally changes him within," but such as he wished to be, such as he wanted to appear to us beyond his century, facing Bonaparte, treating him as man to man, and even making use of him, attaching him to his own destiny: "That man," he wrote, "who envelops me with his tyranny as another might with solitude."

Nevertheless, he could not hide from us; unwittingly he gave us the means to go through appearances to the real man whom we have the weakness to love. Other lives "make a picture," but without the author wanting it; those are the ones that touch me. A thunder-struck Nietzsche in a street in Turin, Arthur Rimbaud returning to die in the Hospital of the Conception, all those who led in the battle of Jacob with the angel, who struggled in the clutches of God, who searched for their truth and who lost themselves in order to find it, it is with those that Chateaubriand must be compared if we

61

wish to put him in his place (not the first certainly), in the ranks of true greatness.

He is the lofty patron of the mediocre man of letters, whose kingdom is of this world. At twenty I was charmed by the cry of the young Barrès: "suffering to the point of clinching his fists with desire to dominate life . . ." Life? No, not only editors, literary cafés and society; Barrès dreamed of power and political domination. Almost everyone failed where Chateaubriand succeeded. Lamartine mounted higher and more quickly, but with waxen wings and, after his fall, dragged himself along, an impecunious old man. If I compare his life to that of the Viscount, how badly compounded it seems to me!

Chateaubriand himself escaped from the library without breaking his back; he escaped the writing-desk in spite of the odious suspicion that men of letters have always inspired in political specialists, whether they are called Louis XVIII, Villèle or Marshal Stalin; and he intervened in their game with destructive power. When Barrès, in *l'Homme Libre*,[1] writes of his hero that: "he admitted in letters only Chateaubriand at the Verona Congress," that quip betrays his deepseated home-sickness for a career which, for him, never went beyond the bays of the Chamber. Barrès, that bee on the edge of the inkstand, that the bungling politicians of the Third Republic, for more than thirty years, pushed back into his ink, without anyone ever having the notion to make him an ambassador to the Vatican! That was because the "free man," having become President of the League of Patriots, under his outward cynicism, remained faithful to his conservative ideas. He was imprisoned by them, while Chateaubriand, his master and model, carried political immoralism to the point of arming himself with his very fidelity in order to bring down the legitimate monarchy.

[1] *The Free Man.* Transl. Note.

René's marvelous violin note, that gave the pitch to the century, should not make us lose sight of the fact that Chateaubriand was a deep man, one of those who do not doubt that there are privileges for geniuses and that the ordinary law, except that of honor, concerns only the ordinary. That Breton cadet belonged to the posterity of Retz which does not serve the state, but which makes use of the state.

The care he took to compose his life is especially noticeable in his art of using fine sentiments (which, moreover, he really felt, just enough not to be hypocritical). He grew up nobly, elbowed his way with grandeur; and his scorn for money, his spectacular resignations, his renunciations were of more use to him than meanness to others. His "ladies," who sometimes helped him with the influential people of the day, never disturbed him in his relationships with God and, after a century, this apologist of Christianity always seems to us to be escorted by charming and passionate shadows, from the unreal Sylphide to the very real Hortense Allart, without it costing him a single admirer from among the virtuous.

His relationships with God . . . That is where Chateaubriand irritates me, not, to be sure, because he was a sinner, nor because he put the last touches to his *Genius of Christianity* at Savigny-sur-Orge, in Madame de Beaumont's bedroom, but because in it he attached no importance to the point of view of Faith, because it is not very certain that his religious convictions were of better alloy than those he professed in politics—and especially because the reasons he has for preaching Christianity, at least at the beginning of his career, are those which have always filled me with disgust, I confess. I care little for religion to be touching if it is not true! The poetry of bells and cloisters, everything by which the young Chateaubriand is charmed, hides from him the Cross where a part of humanity is stretched out, from generation to generation. He who does not sacrifice himself to the Christ, and who sacrifices so many creatures to his greed, seems not to know that religion demands innumerable human sacrifices, and that its beauty would be nothing if it were not "truth's splendor." He forgets that, if false, it would become a snare in which young people would be entrapped by the thousands and that they would continue to be trapped as long as there are men to leave everything and follow a man dead for almost two thousand years because they believe He is the Son of God.

If this Chateaubriand whom I loved so much in my youth, pleases me less to-day, it is because from now on what attaches me to a writer or an artist, is the power he has to surpass himself, to gush forth from the cell of his literary personality. When I was François-René's age at Combourg, no one was more charmed than I by the first harmonies of *Mémoires d'outre-tombe*. At sixteen, René and his passionate sister were among my familiar shadows; and still to-day the *Vie de Rancé* supports my dreams of the lengthening shadow by a muted accompaniment.

That does not prevent the old Chateaubriand, with one foot in the grave, from holding the pose in the bedchamber of Abbaye-aux-Bois, surrounded by adorers and served by Madame Récamier. He keeps it even to the tomb which he has chosen. He thought he would keep it until the end of time, before that almost ever dark sea of which Renan has written that it forms a circle of eternal groans on the horizon. François-René associates with the dust that he has become that eternal weeper who was already weeping the day of his birth ("the tempest whose sound lulled my first sleep . . .").

But did he, who had a presentiment of almost everything about to be born into the world, suspect that human genius would turn to the destruction, not only of the species, but of the planet itself, and that some day there would be nothing so fragile as the granite of his native shore, and that man would need only a few seconds to destroy utterly those banks that, for thousands of years, the ocean had not been able to wear away? Perhaps, after all, he would not have been surprised by it: in regard to that day of days when the Son of Man shall appear, he wrote: "More than once death will swallow up the races, will pour silence over events as the snow fallen during the night silences the rattle of the carts."

This virtuoso of boredom, who almost to the end had appetites to satisfy and who did not fail to do so, this Breton with the determined jaw did not despise anything in life before having assured himself he had obtained everything. He none the less communicated to his century a despair that was, it seems to me, a presentiment. We have come to acknowledge him right, we who no longer are tempted to pose, since nothing remains of the European society before which Chateaubriand assumed the pose that Girodet has arrested.

The "ladies" no longer ornament literary destinies very much; sodomy and erotism have driven them away. Without a doubt there still exist heroic destinies, but the time of assassins has come when the hero turns to the villain and noble deeds resemble crimes. We know above all that what Chateaubriand only half believed perhaps, is true, and that there will not be any posterity. Who would concern himself to-day, as he did, with choosing and marking the spot for his tomb? We belong to a humanity less advanced in civilization than the primitive tribe, since it respects sepulchers no more than cradles.

MAURICE AND EUGÉNIE
DE GUÉRIN

IN 1937, A NUMBER OF US HAD GOTTEN TOGETHER UNDER THE oaks of Cayla in memory of Maurice de Guérin asleep for a century—"of Maurice dead, of Maurice in Heaven." You know that is the dedication inscribed by Eugénie de Guérin at the head of the eleventh notebook of his journal: "Friday, the nineteenth of July, at half past eleven, eternal date!" she had written on the evening of the day on which her brother died. Are there eternal dates? They are all bound up, even in time, with our ephemeral memories.

But those bloody and criminal years that have passed since my last coming to Cayla have been able to do nothing to our fidelity. The fidelity of the heart is stronger than the destructive power of man. Eugénie and Maurice continue to live, and they have become even dearer to us than they were before that tide covered up the world again. There is nothing that our eyes see, nor our ears hear that does not render more sacred that high-place of Cayla, that modest terrace like the one where we played as children, or suffered as adolescents. Yes, a high-place where unfolded a bloody drama too, although the blood remained invisible. How after our own hearts is the Guérinian drama where God, nature, Grace, profane and fraternal love fought for the inspired child.

No other in literary history is comparable to it except, perhaps, that of the Brontës. But what goes on between the Brontë children in the secrecy of a Protestant rectory, seems to us enveloped by a sinister and disturbing light. Here, at Cayla, in the light of definite dogmas, the inflexible gentleness of the Catholic rule holds Eugénie de Guérin bound under our eyes, possessed by a twofold and very pure love: her love for God and her love for Maurice. Here everything is clear; everything is drawn with the scrupulous exactitude of an illuminated design: that girl, noble and poor, who gets up at the shadow of dawn in winter to go to Mass at Andillac, who threads her distaff, explains the catechism to the little boys, helps with the cooking, follows, step by step, what a half century later, another girl, she a Norman, Thérèse de Lisieux, was to call *the narrow way* and which is a way of giving one's life from day to day without any other witness than a hidden God.

For what, for whom give one's life? Emily Brontë, in her Anglican rectory, did not believe she could earn merit for her brother; she did not move, as did Eugénie de Guérin, in that Catholic universe of reversibility where the last among the faithful cooperates with Christ's passion. Eugénie believes that God needs her to save Maurice. She prays for Maurice who does not pray any more, he who formerly was called *the young saint* by the peasants of Andillac, and who lives in Paris, engaged in passions that she feels instinctively and which fill her with dismay.

But she too is possessed by a passion: Eugénie is not a saint like Thérèse; she is not detached. It is that Maurice, for whom she suffers, who binds her with bonds so tender and so violent that she was not to know much in advance (but didn't she always know it?) that it could be he, that adored brother, who, according to the economy of Grace, would be demanded back from her.

To be sure, we know that she loved him only in God and for God. The heart-rending cry of her journal, the day after her brother's death, expresses all we could say on the subject: "Oh, my dear! Maurice, Maurice, are you far from me! Do you hear me? What is it like where you are now? You see that I am waiting; you possess what I hope; you know what I only believe."

But it still remains that she was terribly attached to him. What was the nature of that love of Eugénie for Maurice? One must always come back to Lacordaire's words: "There is only one love." What are called the ties of blood that create between brothers and sisters a union often very close, is not the love, that very pure love that Eugénie had for Maurice, as free of all sexuality as love can be, but a love of flesh and blood just the same. It is Maurice himself, it is Maurice's body that, until her last breath, Eugénie will hold on her lap, like a very frail Pietà. It is of that poor flesh she dreams, on August 31, 1839, five weeks after the burial: "It is raining. This rain which brings green to the meadows and woods falls on the earth that covers you, and dissolves your remains in the cemetery yonder in Andillac." In a letter, she recalls to Barbey d'Aurevilly what he said to her on the day of Maurice's marriage, during the wedding breakfast: "How handsome your brother is!" Eighteen months sooner, when Maurice was still alive, and had returned to Paris after a stay at Cayla, Eugénie went into his room which he had just left: There are your shoes under the table, the table still arranged, the mirror hanging from its nail, the books you were reading yesterday evening before going to sleep, and I who kissed you, touched you, saw you. What kind of a world is it where everything disappears? Maurice, Oh! how I need both you and God!

"How I need both you and God!" That is the cry of

Eugénie's heart . . . But is it an accident if, in that cry, God comes after Maurice? You understand very well that I am not trying to disparage Eugénie, but on the contrary to bring her closer to us. Would we love her as we do love her if she had, from the beginning, been the saint stripped of everything that she was when she passed into eternity? She needed years which continued long after the death of Maurice to attain that penury.

And yet she remained separated from the living Maurice most of her life. Eugénie de Guérin's journal would suffice to render us conscious of what we already know by experience: that there is nothing less necessary than physical presence to encourage love. The great Bossuet was not very expert in the matter, he who saw in flight the only efficacious arm against passion! That negation of absence which it proclaims on every page, is not the least of the beauties of Eugénie's journal. One could not carry further than she the determination to live heart to heart with someone who is not there. That total occupation of a being by another being from whom one is separated by hundreds of miles, that is the whole journal of Eugénie de Guérin.

And it is doubtless with Maurice's soul that she believes herself concerned; it is that soul that she must return to God, at all costs. Her sincerity is not questionable; that is what she wants, that is what she thinks she wants. But to return Maurice to God is to separate him from a world strange to Eugénie, hostile to Eugénie, it is to reintegrate him into that universe which was theirs, it is for herself that she unwittingly struggles while she fights for God. To return Maurice to the God of his childhood, to the God present in the little church at Andillac, that is to defeat Paris, the adversary with a thousand faces; that is, for Eugénie, to become again the elder sister, sole and sovereign mistress of that fraternal soul.

That is what the holy girl is not conscious of, doubtless. Since Maurice is not there, it is around Maurice's soul that all that very pure but too human love is crystallized. Oh! without a doubt, Eugénie counts first on prayer and sacrifice to reconquer him. But she does not always refrain from urging him with words, insisting in season and out of season at the risk of annoying and irritating him. If passion did not blind her, Eugénie would see and understand that no one has ever converted anyone, that we are sometimes the instruments of Grace, that we sometimes find the moment when it is necessary to hold out our hand to a soul. But nothing more! How can she hope, poor girl at Cayla, that her reasoning could unknot the crisis of a young being wholly ensnared in the great pantheistic temptation of the century, and whom Cybele is drawing to the antipodes of Calvary, and turning away from that cross on which he already knows that in a time not far distant in his destiny, he will have to stretch himself. But not yet! Not at once!

In the thickest of the drama, Eugénie wanders a little blindly, it seems to me, gropingly going across the stormy zones of Maurice's passion for the Baroness de Maistre, his friendship for Barbey d'Aurevilly, his dangerous liaisons, his desires and his dreams.

As long as he was but a child, she had only one heart with him. Now that he has become a man full of secrets and enigmas, Eugénie continues to demand that their two lots be interwoven. Is there not something or other devouring in such a love? A sister who does not marry (especially at a time when outside of marriage and the cloister there was no imaginable life for a girl of that little provincial world), a sister who does not marry, is often a woman who, having renounced her own history and private drama, tries to maintain herself in the center of the life of her brother whom she cherishes, of that stranger in whom, with tenacious passion, she tries to resuscitate the child she has nursed on her lap. "My future is bound to yours, they are brothers," she insisted, on November 17, 1834.

From the terrace of Cayla, Eugénie tried to capture the indecipherable messages of a fine vessel carried along by the sea—messages that he himself intentionally makes indecipherable. Shall I tell all? It is Maurice who here appears to be the most affected, the most deeply wounded, Maurice who is nearing death, weighed down by all the secrets he is concealing and who is putting off the scent Eugénie, Caro, his fiancée, and the Baroness de Maistre, strange heart scattered between two worlds, torn by all those beings who live only through him. But he, of what does he die? I am thinking of a rather absurd line (I think it is by François Coppée):

He was dying of the disease of a too beloved child . . .

a line which suddenly becomes beautiful and echoes deep within us if we apply it to Maurice de Guérin. "Maurice is sad," wrote Caro, the Indian fiancée, to Eugénie. "He has a depth of sadness that I am trying to dispel. I read it in his eyes . . ." We know why he was sad and that he did not love that girl into the arms of whom he was letting himself be thrown although he loved someone else . . . Did he really love Madame de Maistre? To tell the truth, perhaps he was only attracted by those elementary forces in which, despairingly, he aspired to lose himself, he who compared his thought to a fire in the sky that trembles on the horizon between two worlds.

Just the same Eugénie perceives that intermingling of passions; she guesses; we feel that she is burning: "Perhaps I am mistaken," she writes on the same date, "but it seems to me that I see in you something that is poisoning you, that will kill you if you do not free yourself from it . . ." By a natural movement of that pious soul, she brings everything back to the same idea that her brother's conversion would cure him. She does not know that Grace does not destroy nature, that it could only superadd itself, by illuminating it, to that of Maurice. "If I could only see you a Christian!" she groaned. "I would give my life and all for that." Does Eugénie dream that God will take her at her word perhaps? She declares herself ready to give all for Maurice's salvation . . . but if all were going to be asked of her? and not her own life which she does not want, but her brother's which is dearer to her than life? Who knows if it is not Eugénie's prayer that is going to hasten the end of Maurice's lot? One could say that God's pity prepares the unhappy sister for it: she has forebodings, dreams from which nothing in that Cayla isolated from the world diverts her. How pathetic this contrast makes her journal!—the contrast between a life in which nothing happens except the birth of a lamb, the death of a bird, or a snowfall during the night, and the marvelous power of that imprisoned love powerless to fly to the one whose body and soul, two hundred miles from there, are attacked at the very sources of life: "A little reading, a little writing, a few glances at the rain, that is my day. At night, in my dreams, I see your bed in flames. What do these terrors that you cause me by day and night mean? Oh! that at least I do not have to worry about your health! The rest is enough, God only knows."

We too know that rest which God knows: it is Maurice's indifference to eternal matters. "*Holy pleasures from Heaven, adorable ideas* . . ." That line from Polyeuctus could be inscribed at the head of all Eugénie's notebooks. But Maurice is carried along toward other ideas which are not adorable; he aspires to pleasures that are not holy. And his body, like his soul, is a prey to death. Eugénie knows it; she hears him coughing across the miles that separate them: "To be in Paris, in a room alongside of yours, as here, so as to hear your breath, sleep, cough. Oh! I hear all that, but across five hundred miles. Oh! distances, distances!"

"Friday, July 19, at half past eleven, eternal date!" Now that her brother is dead, Eugénie probably believes that she has paid the whole price asked and that she is entering into the peace of total destitution. Outwardly, what is there left for her to give? She has lost the only being who really counted for her in this world. But she has lots to learn still about that love of God in whom she trusts. Unattached from a human viewpoint, she is not yet so according to Grace. It still remains for her to penetrate the sense of a word she has not known, the one that Saint Angela of Foligno heard one day: "It is not to make you laugh that I have loved you." The very humble Eugénie de Guérin is called to a higher perfection than she imagines. It seems natural to her to remain attached to Maurice dead, as closely and, on a very elevated plane, in as fleshly a way as when she was separated from him only by miles of highway. The landscapes of Cayla grip Maurice: "You know, my friend," he had written one day, "the charm of steps taken over beloved traces . . ." The beloved traces of Maurice are everywhere about here: there is a certain point on the horizon that Eugénie prefers because she remembers that Maurice's glance rested on it. But more than in nature, she rediscovers her brother in beings, and particularly in the friend who was dearest of all to him, Barbey d'Aurevilly, and then in the woman he loved. The journal that Eugénie wrote for Maurice, she agrees to continue for that dissolute young man, for that Barbey who would only inspire remoteness in her: was it not he who initiated Maurice

into that Parisian life that she judged iniquitous? Maurice
at La Chesnaie, near Lamennais, then at Val d'Arguenon,
with Hippolyte de la Morvonnais, was already a child ensnared by Cybele, but he still belonged to Christ. It was Barbey d'Aurevilly who drew out from the dowdy little country
bumpkin that dandy charming as a vignette by Tony Johannot, whose "profile of the last of the Abencerages" disturbed
so many hearts. It was Barbey d'Aurevilly who led him into
little debauches, far from the peace of God. Now it is not
enough to say that Eugénie held no grudge against that dex-
terous Barbey d'Aurevilly.

Nevertheless, she discovered, with a mixture of joy and
sorrow, that in her brother, the poet had appeared admirable
to other eyes than hers, that the slightest words he wrote were
hunted out, received, and that this young deceased was perhaps going to live in the memory of mankind. The posthumous
fame of Maurice links his sister to life once more. It is of that
fame that she talks indefinitely with the Baroness de Maistre
who every day recites for Maurice the service for the dead.
Thus four hundred miles are joined, mingled, and weave a
net around that soul returned to the world. They will have
to be broken one by one, all consolation turned to bitterness,
but even that is not enough; she will have to know desertion,
betrayal, calumny and scorn. In that chalice she thought
she had emptied at her brother's death she has left the dregs.

She will not lie down to die until she has drunk the last
drop.

The first blow that strikes her comes from the direction
she least expected it. The poem, *The Centaur*, that the *Revue
des Deux Mondes* publishes she admires, to be sure, but she
did not know it before the others; Maurice had not shown
it to her. Probably he was afraid she would not like the pagan
intoxication very much, that odor of crushed leaves and sap

in the forest full of desires. But there is something worse: it
was George Sand who extolled Maurice in the review, "that
woman," as Eugénie always designates her, that woman she
would detest and despise if hatred and scorn were permitted a
Christian, that woman who for all eternity fixes the image of
a Maurice de Guérin, captive of Cybele. That Attis chained to
his dreams, that savage Endymion, is not the child she carried
in her arms, nor the young saint of Cayla, not Lamennais'
disciple; it is not the one she saw on the eve of his death,
adoring the little host of the tabernacle of Andillac that had
come to help him in his last agony. We have been present at
the same misunderstanding around other remains; in the same
way we argued twenty years ago at the coffin of our friend
Jacques Rivière. Sad arguments where both sides are right
and wrong, because a Christian artist, turn and turn about,
gives hostages to Grace and to nature and because he wears
himself out trying to reconcile the irreconcilable, until finally,
as happened in the case of Maurice de Guérin and Jacques
Rivière, all conflict is appeased in the light of the last hour.

So the posthumous fame of Maurice became more bitter
than gall to Eugénie. That Maurice whom men revived, the
savage Centaur, is not the baptized child she cherishes, and
by whom she was cherished, and who lives forever in the light
of love.

I shall not linger over the final trials that were to over-
whelm Eugénie. Even a century after, I should fear to touch
on the secrets of that very pure heart, especially at that Cayla
filled with his dear presence. Barbey d'Aurevilly was not only
fickle and cruel; there are silences that are crimes, such as
the one he opposed to Eugénie. As for the Baroness de Maistre
who drove her away after having humiliated her without
reason and without excuse, it will be her chastisement that we
denounce her to-day, she who could have survived and ap-

peared to us in all the glory of the love she inspired in Maurice. It is pitiful to see Eugénie de Guérin, that noble girl not devoid of passion to be sure, nor probably of clumsiness, but absolutely upright, caught in the intrigues and little abominations of the world. There is something gratuitous and supernatural in that sudden ferocity of the great lady, as in the incomprehensible silence of Barbey d'Aurevilly.

But now, on coming back to Cayla, Eugénie de Guérin has the right to say to God: "You only." Her father, another brother, a sister and some nephews are the anchors that hold her to this terrace for a little while. There she is at last ready, that fiery soul in which everything is consumed that is not God. There she is, waiting for the blessed death that arrived on May 31, 1848, on the eve of Ascension. She must rejoice to-day because, in order to celebrate the centenary of that blessed death, all of us, his friends and the Académie française that I have the honor to represent here, have chosen the eighteenth of July, the eve of the day on which Maurice closed his eyes to the beauty of the world. It is the sign that we do not separate them in our hearts and that, as they are joined forever, our affection continues here below to mingle their two shadows, which are no longer in pain, their two souls eternally at peace.

BALZAC

ONE DAY A BOY OF FIFTEEN, NAMED PAUL BOURGET, ENtered a reading-room on the rue Soufflot and asked for the first volume of *Père Goriot*. It was one o'clock when he began reading. It was seven when the young Paul was once more in the street having finished the entire work. "The hallucination of that reading was so strong," writes Bourget, "that I staggered . . . The intensity of the dream into which Balzac had plunged me produced effects on me similar to those of alcohol or opium. I stayed a few minutes taking in the reality of the things about me and my own poor reality . . ."

Chance had opened for him the door through which it is most convenient to penetrate into *The Human Comedy*. Not that Goriot dominates Balzac's work, but that novel seems to me to be its focal-point. At that point begin the great avenues he has traced in the density of his forest of men. The Vauquer home into which we are introduced on the first pages, that "middle-class boarding-house" whose musty, rancid odor will follow us for a long time after we have closed the book, that evil-smelling dining-room with its pigeon-holes where the boarders put their soiled napkins, that is the nest from which Balzac's characters, who are going to serve us as guides, take flight. From now on, it will be enough for us to attach ourselves to them from volume to volume in order to

77

tie up the threads of all the mingled destinies of which the plot of *The Human Comedy* is composed.

Of Goriot's two daughters, one, Delphine de Nucingen, introduces us to the financial world; the other, Madame de Festaud, mistress of the formidable Maxime de Trailles, opens the doors of high society for us, and precedes us to the home of the Viscountess de Beauséant. The young Eugène de Rastignac, "Mama" Vauquer's boarder, is one of the finest birds of prey in an age when claws grow, that the provinces let loose on Paris, and one whose implacability and grace Balzac adores. The great doctor in *The Human Comedy*, the one whom Balzac, according to legend, called in during his last agony, the celebrated Bianchon, is here still only a studious and underfed medical student. But it is especially Vautrin, the convict, who appears to us for the first time in *Goriot* whose meeting holds import for us; it is he, the outlaw, who holds all the secrets, all the passwords for Balzac's universe. With him we find ourselves in the center of the immense canvas; behind this leading man, we can start out without danger of getting lost.

Perhaps a work like *Eugénie Grandet*, for instance, would disconcert a "beginner" less. But it is just because *Goriot* does not attain perfection and that in it we come up against an essential fault of Balzac, that it seems to us excellent to choose it as a lode-stone, in order to judge whether the neophyte possesses a leaning toward Balzac or not. I know fine minds that the character of Goriot exasperates. Let them go no further, or at least let them resign themselves to the multiplication, under their feet, of subjects of irritation.

Père Goriot really belongs to the kind of character that, in *The Human Comedy*, stands out only because of the gross exaggeration of a trait. He is not *a father*, he is *the father*. Thanks to the detailed knowledge we have of his outward

appearance, thanks especially to that rooting in the squalor
of the Vauquer house, he gives us the illusion of being real.
The fetid smells that Balzac makes us breath in, force us to
admit the physical existence of this type and gives an appearance of life to that "Christ of paternity."

In order to paint him, the author started out with the individual possessing the most personality and the best defined:
a retired business-man who has sacrificed everything to his
two daughters to whom he offers idolatrous worship. From
that old man, Balzac draws, little by little, the picture of a
custom-made being, denatured, lofty to the point of hebetude,
buckling with his own hands the silver that he still has, in
order that his "Nasie" can pay with those ingots, the debts of
her lover, Maxime de Trailles, "a man capable of ruining
orphans." According as we are won over or repelled by that
"typified" individual we yield to or resist, more or less
quickly, the hoodoo of Balzac.

But in *Goriot*, as it happens, we get acquainted with the
character who is located at the antipodes of the father-
martyr: Vautrin, the convict, although he too, characterized
with scrupulous art as to his physical appearance, has no real
existence at the beginning; a romantic hero of secondary importance, a character dreamed up and not observed, but
whom Balzac nourishes little by little with his inhibited desires, with his taste for domination and with all that an-
nounces Nietzsche in his nature; and Vautrin, from chapter
to chapter, becomes individualized, incarnated and at length
vibrates with a terrible life. He draws away from the idea and
the abstract vision in which he had his origin, and by an in-
verse phenomenon, in proportion as Goriot rises to a type, he
goes down, touches the earth and finally becomes a person,
an individualized type.

Not that he altogether resembles a being of flesh and blood

hardened in common clay; he is a forerunner of the Nietzschean superman. He delivers from obscure and unmention-
able demons and incarnates passions without a face. Here
the novelist goes beyond experience and gives life to a creature whose blood-kin we will never encounter among humans.
Vautrin avenges the man of letters, lost in debt, cheated,
tracked, misunderstood by critics, a dupe of the Duchess of
Castries and la Polonaise for whom he finally exhausts himself and who lets him die alone, a convict himself whom the
slave-traders exploit.

Vautrin (his real name is Jacques Collin), twice escaped
from prison and lurking in the shadow of the Vauquer house,
incubates the young Rastignac in the hope of dominating the
world by his intervention. What he will obtain later from the
handsome Lucien de Rubempré (in *Lost Illusions*) Rastignac,
conscientious and crafty at the same time, refuses him. But
from *Goriot* on, we perceive the abysses in which Balzac is
satisfied to dream. A writer does not confide either in his correspondence or even in his personal diary. His creatures alone
relate his true history, the one he did not live, perhaps, but
that he wanted to live. As Lucien de Rubempré, by a strange
reversibility, makes Vautrin taste every kind of intoxication,
Vautrin delivers Balzac's disciple of Napoléon and precursor
of Nietzsche—that Balzac, whom already during his life, the
conservatives took to themselves (the Fitz-Jameses, the Castries and the Abrantès), that diplomatic apologist for Christianity who, in his heart, like almost all peers, vindicates the
indefeasible right of superior individuals to follow only a
morality cut to fit them.

No prospector of *The Human Comedy* has yet dared to reveal the very depths of the subjects of every sort that Balzac
has dared to touch upon and pursue boldly, long before André
Gide and Marcel Proust. But from *Goriot* on, the neophyte

reader bathes in an immoralism beside which what one reproaches in today's writers can be found in the Bibliothèque
Rose.[1] Balzac is the historian of a society which, saved from
the Revolution, is looking for satiety first. All the more, because under the reign of the Congregation, Christian faith is
dead in the depths of many hearts where all the passions are
awake unmuzzled. Diplomatic Catholicism alone imposes upon
them some forms, some prudence; good-breeding, too, and
courtesy and manners that have survived the emigration
cover up and conceal the tracks of the wild beasts.

The young Bourget on the threshold of the reading-room
on the rue Soufflot staggered because he was drunk with the
most bitter knowledge; the child had eaten of the fruit of the
tree. He was no longer ignorant of the extremes to which
filial ingratitude can go, nor of the savagery of people of the
world, nor of the ways by which a small-town young man can
become corrupted in his heart, nor of the underworld of the
prisons, nor of the meanness of certain persons outwardly virtuous, such as that Michonneau who turns Vautrin over to
the police. And he alone, the convict, dominates that repul-
sive society with his formidable shoulders.

More closely attached to the powers of the flesh than any
of the wild young dandies that people his books, we still know
that Balzac was able to light up *The Human Comedy* with a
supernatural light. The author of *Louis Lambert, The Country Doctor* and *The Other Side of Contemporary History*
knew everything; he had a foreboding of everything, even of
that subterranean river, of that current of Grace that flows
invisible through the world. His universe, the most iniquitous
that a human brain has ever conceived, seems glowing with
spirituality if it is compared with that of his miserable satel-
lites (with that of Zola, for instance). But none of that flame

[1] Publication of highly moral tone, intended for young girls. Transl. note.

is yet burning in *Goriot*, unless Goriot himself, devoured alive by his two daughters, appears lofty to the reader (what Balzac probably hoped). Let us confess that, in our eyes, that blind, stuttering worship, that absurd idolatry, escapes all nobility and has no part in grandeur. The hero of *Goriot* is not the half-witted Goriot, but Vautrin covered with guilt.

Balzac doubtless thought so as, in the last chapter, he burdens Eugène de Rastignac with bringing out the moral of the book. Mingling with the servants of his two murderous daughters, he follows the old man's funeral procession. Balzac shows him to us alone at Père-Lachaise, leaning over the tomb "where he buried his last tear of a young man." And then there are the words: "It is up to us two now!" cast at the city by the ambitious youth, a challenge that so many French adolescents have repeated from generation to generation.

"He returned on foot the rue d'Artois and went to dine with Madame de Nucingen!" That is the last sentence in the book, the most cruel and the one that opens to the neophyte perspectives of a world savage but full of delight, into which he may be permitted to enter without leaving his room, and whose passions he can live over again in his mind, a pleasure in which there is collaboration with what has since been called human geography, since Balzac's humanity is closely united with our provinces described as to their physical appearance and their customs, and since fiction goes hand in hand at every instant with great history.

But at the same time that *Goriot* is a sort of psychological focal point in *The Human Comedy*, it attaches us firmly to its geographical center, that Paris lying twisted along the banks of the Seine, and more than to any other quarter, to that inaccessible quarter that holds sway between the column Vendome and the dome of the Invalides.

In Balzac, the most mediocre passions rise to his height;

so, when it is a question of his heroes or himself, *snobbism,* as it is called to-day, loses all its character of meanness. It is true that under the Restoration the Salons still retain political power, and that the pleasures with which they flatter the vanity of an ambitious youth always precede more substantial conquests.

There was a time when Balzac's great ladies made society laugh, and even critics, like Emile Faguet, who thought they knew all about duchesses. To-day, the reader of *Goriot* does not find them so funny. Delphine de Nucingen, Anastasie de Restaud and the Viscountess de Beauséant are not the least lifelike among all those who fill *The Human Comedy* with their passions, hypocritical or avowed, and of whom Balzac has not ignored a single expression. The Duchess de Castries could play with the poor fat, gap-toothed, illustrious man; but it is she, in the last analysis, who, under the features of the Duchess de Langeais, will remain, thanks to him, our eternal plaything.

Balzac escaped Vautrin's curse; in order to know women of the world he did not need to cut himself in two, nor enjoin a Rastignac or a Rubempré to be happy for him. He did not love Madame de Berny; he was not loved by anyone in between. His "delecta," although twenty years older than he, enriched him with more passion than he would have needed to light up all the love affairs in his books. To almost all, even to the youths and courtesans like Coralie or Esther, Madame de Berny communicated that power of renunciation of an aged mistress, who stifles every moan and asks nothing except to keep until death her humble place at the knees of the grownup child whom she still watches over with a maternal eye now that, for the whole universe, he has become this brilliant genius.

Balzac was adored, literally, and all, his feminine psychology bears the mark of that adoration. To tell the truth, everywhere and at every level of *The Human Comedy*, God's place is usurped. This usurpation is affirmed already on every page of *Goriot*. Considered under this aspect, Balzac's work appears essentially anti-Christian. It already offers a Nietzschean refusal to Christ's question: "What will it serve a man to gain the whole world if he lose his own soul"? Balzac's humanity, born under the sign of Bonaparte, protests there is nothing to do in the world but gain the universe. In its entirety and apart from some admirable figures, it does not believe that it has a soul. A world without a soul is that of the Marsays and the Trailles; and Eugène de Rastignac himself, in order to become one of them, must first renounce his.

But what we advance in regard to his creatures, we take good care not to say of the creator himself. It is evident that Balzac learned from his own heroes that Catholicism is necessary to subdue the human animal, and we know, too, what he received in this respect from Bonald and Maistre. But his religious thought goes deeper; full of contradictions and waverings, it must be followed in all its meanderings from childhood. The personal relationships that a man has kept up with Christ, and that constitute the most secret part of his life, are almost never approached. For Balzac, it could not be *Goriot* at any rate, that could orient us in that direction of our research. Every one of the beings that the Vauquer house hatches out between its sticky walls, nourished some greed, is bent on some particular trail and never gives up his quest to look at the Heavens. There is scarcely a one who does not put the infinite into creatures or into the possession of the most materialistic goods, almost none who is not resolved to go even as far as crime. Each one seems to have understood in advance (but on giving it its basest meaning) that entreaty of Zarathustra: "I beg you, remain faithful to the earth."

GUSTAVE FLAUBERT

O NE JANUARY DAY IN 1844, ON THE WAY TO PONT-
Audemer, the first attack of a terrible malady struck
Gustave Flaubert down in the cabriolet he was driving. That
day, his youth received a mortal blow. Although he was only
twenty-two, the child-wonder whom we evoke in the unknown
Trouville of that time, with his red flannel shirt, his trousers
of coarse blue cloth and his scarf pulled tightly across his
back, was struck down. Later, he himself dared to write
Louise Colet: "I was wonderful, I can say it now, sufficiently
so as to attract the eyes of an entire auditorium, as happened
to me at Rouen, on the opening night of Ruy Blas . . ."

Just as Pascal tried to see in illness "the natural state of
the Christian," so the young Flaubert was going to find in it
a privation from sensual pleasure, a limit to the demands of
his heart. He owed to it the power he had to give himself entirely to Art, to the jealous idol he had begun to adore when
he was only a high-school boy on the quais of Rouen.

So at twenty-two, he will no longer speak of his youth except as of a death. It seems to flame up a few more years, as
long as his sister Caroline and his friend Alfred Le Poitevin
live. It is they who will carry away the remains with them
into death. On March 20, 1846, Caroline dies. The boyish
laughter and outbursts will never sound again. "Yesterday,
at eleven o'clock, we buried the poor girl. They put on her

85

wedding dress with the clusters of roses, everlastings and violets; I passed the night in vigil . . ."

That very year, one last love is going to upset his life. But the feeling he avows for Louise Colet in no way recalls the adolescent passion that formerly made him dream at Madame Schlesinger's feet; throughout this intrigue, he remains a sick man, using his nerves to observe and explore himself; and above all a fanatical worshipper of the sentence, who would not sacrifice one word for a kiss. Poor Louise Colet, she hardly counted as soon as Madame Bovary was in the balance! Art served first. Neglected, she had many times to reread the first letters she received from the young provincial, the only ones in which a heart possessed really beats: "Now the night is warm and soft; I hear the great tulip-tree under my window tremble in the wind . . ." And the other letter of the ninth of April, 1846 ". . . I hear the sailors singing as they pull up anchor to leave with the tide. Not a cloud nor a breath of air. The river is white under the moon, black in the shadow. The butterflies play around my candles and the perfume of the night comes in through my open window. And you, are you asleep?" But some lines further he warns her already! "You thought I was young, and I am old."

He himself does not know how right he is; someone is going away, carrying with him what remained of his youth; Alfred Le Poitevin married. Gustave repeats to Louise Colet: "Love art rather than me . . . prefer the idea . . ." But with his friend, he did not even think of separating art or idea from their mutual affection. Such is the privilege of friendship that it is enriched by reading together, by spiritual discoveries and even by boredom shared. Art, which had united the friends, separated the lovers. Louise Colet's handsome face must have darkened the day she received this confidence: "The greatest events of my life have been a few thoughts, readings and certain sunsets at Trouville, at the seashore and chats for five or six consecutive hours with a friend who is now married and lost to me." He was lost, but he was living. Alfred Le Poitevin dies during the night of April third and fourth, 1848. On the seventh, Flaubert sends Maxime du Camp the account of his last moments, his death and burial. What a page! In Flaubert's entire work, we would search in vain for another which surpasses it in magnificence.

Le Poitevin's youth had been better protected against suffocation than Flaubert's; nature, which that pantheist worshipped, protected him half-way. As the window was open and the sun streaming into the room, the dying young man cried out: "Close it; it is too beautiful! It is too beautiful!" For Flaubert, too, the window is closed henceforth.

Probably before his final retirement, he had one last, magnificent outing, his trip to the Orient. But everything there bores him and already, as though he were an old man, only the past counts. Not that he is dried up; on that point, his letters to his mother reassure us. How deeply we are moved by the tender little-boy accent that the young giant finds again when he writes to "his poor darling," to his "dear old mama," to his "poor old adored mama!" In that huge correspondence, it is impossible not to be struck by the subterranean current of tenderness and childish weakness. A certain sentence of the old man's corresponds to another that he did not remember having written forty years sooner; for man's heart does not change much; it does not undulate, it only swirls and eddies, always in the same way, against secret obstacles. After having read the words addressed to his mother on the eve of his departure for Egypt: "You are probably asleep now, poor old darling. How you must have cried tonight, and I, too, shame on us! . . . Oh! how hard I shall kiss you when I come back, poor old mama!" after those tender words of 1849, we must read those written to his niece about thirty years later, in 1876 (his mother had been dead for a long time): "What have become of my poor mother's shawl and garden-hat? Where have you put them? I like to see and touch them from time to time . . ." And in another letter: "I was wrong; it was not the shawl I was looking for but an old green fan that Mama used during our trip to Italy . . ." Such were the sad and secret pleasures of that terrible man, that kind of brute, who scandalized the Goncourts.

In the course of that last excursion, that last escape to the Orient, before shutting himself up until death in the sanctuary of the idol, the traveler enjoys his present youth less than he recalls his ended adolescence. When at dawn, he leaves the house of the courtesan, Rachiouk Hânem, it is not pictures of pleasure that obsess him, but the memory of another morning at the Marchioness de Pommereu's, after a ball: "I had not gone to bed, and in the morning, I had gone boating on the pond, all alone, in my school clothes. The swans watched me pass, and the leaves of the bushes fell into the water. It was a few days before the opening of school and I was fifteen . . ."

That dawn became sunrise and then it was morning, and now the time was at hand for confinement until death and to choose words, to "bawl" them out, to go hunting for assonances. It is not a question of a simple vocation but of a total gift. Even if he were not ill, his passion is great enough to detach him from everything that is not the mania for writing, of everything that stands in its way: wife, family, business. He rejects both the creatures and the Creator; he identifies himself with his work. Monstrous to the point of calling himself a "man-pen"; he lives for his pen, on account of it and in relationship to it. That is a remark from 1852, but he writes similar ones at the end of his life. Especially on that plane, he remains from adolescence to old age, submissive to the same law, incredibly autonomous.

Now nothing will change in his life any more. Here he is enclosed in the study at Croisset, leaning over the green cloth of his work-table, and the rainy wind behind the windows stirs the big tulip-tree. Every word represents a letter; every sentence a defeat or a triumph. He does not hide from himself that this conception of art is, properly speaking, mystical: "I lead an arid life, empty of all outward joy, in which I have nothing to support me except a kind of permanent rage that sometimes weeps with impotence, but which is continual. I love my work with a frantic and depraved love; as an ascetic does the hair-shirt that scratches his abdomen. Sometimes when I find myself empty, when the expression refuses to come, when, after having scratched long pages, I discover I haven't written a sentence, I fall down on my couch, and I remain dazed in an inner morass of weariness . . ." Important text in which both the grandeur and the misery of Flaubert burst forth at the same time. But before criticizing, a writer of our times should first bow his head; hasty and slap-dash production, advertising, speculation as to the de luxe copies, everything that brings dishonor on the literary life of to-day, forces me to speak of Flaubert, even if we did not love him, with deference and respect. Excess for excess, the worship of art should inspire more indulgence than its exploitation.

However, Flaubert's fault is serious, too. Art substituted for God leads him into dangerous paths as a flouted and despised art could not have done. It is not unintentionally that he makes use of mystical language to paint his life devoted to literary work. Knowingly, he usurps the place of the Infinite Being, not for himself probably, but for that continuation of himself, his work: *Bovary, Salammbô,* his charm and his torment. For if he is acquainted with the painful struggles of the saints, he is still better acquainted with the enjoyments that ape the pleasure of the Christians. Flaubert, too, sheds Pascal's tears of joy: "I had moved myself as I wrote. I enjoyed sheer delight in both the emotion and the idea, and in the sentence that caused it, and in the satisfaction of having found it." Here Flaubert forces us to think of the satisfactions of which Saint Theresa writes: "they make flow tears of sorrow of which it could be said they were born of some passion . . ." And so that no doubt may remain as to the total reversal of the values which he accomplishes, further on he describes to us "those emotions without tears, loftier yet," which, he affirms, surpass virtue in moral beauty. He arrives at the point of imitating the extreme ways of the mystical life; and, just as the saints have carried the mania for renunciation to the point of not even asking for Heaven any more, he lifts himself up to "a state of soul superior to life for which glory would be nothing, and happiness itself useless." After having suffered over his work for years, he assures us he loses interest in it, once the manuscript has been given to the publisher. His god requires indifference to all sensuous joy, absolute renunciation. Flaubert's whole destiny is contained in that forgery.

Metaphysics, morality, science, what does he not subordinate to esthetics? In the gloomy study at Croisset, a life is wasting away in the reading of thousands of volumes. Flaubert swallows up everything that touches on philosophy, religion, history, mechanics and applied arts, not to learn anything, nor to retain it, were it even a spark of the truth in some field, but to transform this immense acquisition into nightmares and false ideas with which he will stuff the brains of Saint Anthony, Bouvard and Pécuchet! He never tries to find out whether, among the booty brought back from his readings, hidden under the valueless scrap-iron, there does not gleam a pearl of great price. The effort of the centuries ends up at these caricatures. No idea has value in itself, no discovery. How we are irritated by this stupid brewing of all human acquisition for the creation of two grinning characters!

Doubtless, Bouvard and Pécuchet should not make us forget Charles and Emma Bovary, or Madame Arnoux, or the *Coeur Simple*. Thank Heavens, it was only at the end of his life that Flaubert attained the heights of absurdity. That was because art, his idol, had one important and fortunate exigency: life had to be observed first; this alone was demanded of the artist: to represent reality, what he observed of reality; and, in obedience to this commandment, Flaubert found the secret of his great works. But he only practiced it half-way; a defect in his mentality made him see only the outward appearance of his beings. What existed for him was that collection of pretensions, mannerisms, manias, an attitude that first strikes us in a man, and by which La Bruyère profits. But La Bruyère, justly admired and loved by Flaubert, points out the road to the novelist; he does not lead the way; he remains on the human periphery which horrifies Flaubert but holds him back, and this horror blinds him and prevents him from advancing.

The Bourgeois, that *bête noire* which was poisoning his life, interposes itself between his eye and what he is looking at. He does not believe in that part of immortality which his ridiculous heroes contain within themselves. It is almost in spite of him that the soul of Madame Bovary or Madame Arnoux breaks through sometimes. He thinks he is representing life, and he cuts off everything that does not stir up his nerves. He sees only what excites and nourishes his phobia until, in the excess of his distaste, he turns aside from that horrible world and takes refuge in the evolutions and restoration of abolished races: "Few people will guess how depressed I had to be to undertake to resuscitate Carthage," he writes. "That was a thebaid to which disgust for modern life drove me . . ." For he seems to think sometimes that no trace of all that he loathed in modern man was to be found among the ancients. The author of *Salammbô*, for his own greater happiness, sets up a universe without bourgeoisie, just as Renan, at the same epoch created, out of whole cloth, a Greece of professors and wise men, harmonious and reasonable. These scrupulous historians accumulate documents, and what they finally construct, are myths their own size; they relieve the passions of their souls.

But Flaubert was born clear-sighted and the Greek mirage hardly duped him long: "The gloom of the ancients seems more profound to me than that of moderns . . . No outcries, convulsions, nothing but the rigidity of a thoughtful countenance. The gods being no more, and Christ not yet having come into being, there was a moment between Cicero and Marcus Aurelius when man alone existed." Flaubert, disappointed in the ancients, kept coming back to the bourgeoisie, because his artistic conscience would not give him any rest until he was again resigned to observing life.

Since he could no longer escape the study of the modern Prudhomme, well, he would look the beast in the face; he would take the bull by the horns; that huge bourgeois nonsense would become the subject of his book; he would incarnate it; that would be his masterpiece, he thought. Flaubert creates his nightmare with his own hands. The Bourgeois, under the guise of Bouvard and Pécuchet, sits down to his table, lies down in his bed, fills his days and nights, and ends by taking him by the throat. The Bourgeois has his skin at last; he has literally assassinated Flaubert. The alchemist of Croisset died a victim of the experiments he tried on the human creature; he eliminated the soul of the composite human being to obtain folly in its pure state; it asphyxiated him. Poor Flaubert who said: "Madame Bovary is myself . . ." Did he not know that Bouvard and Pécuchet were as like him as brothers? Why, yes! And he confesses: "Is it the beginning of softening of the brain? Bouvard and Pécuchet fill me to such a point that I have become one with them! Their folly is mine, and I am dying of it." He also believed in the printed page, had faith in text-books, put his confidence in those who know. He who claimed to be horrified by his times, how he obeyed all those pass-words of the "princes of science"! No one was more obedient than he to the intellectual ways of the times. Like a good pupil, he recited Michelet's and Renan's lessons. He thought he was very strong, but he lacked the critical mind. To be truthful, he had only reflexes and rejected only what vexed him. He reacted much more than he reasoned. Certain contacts gave him goose-flesh but he welcomed without resistance the doctrines imposed.

Flaubert is the victim of an anti-Christian era that calumniated the human being. There is not a doubt that, sometimes, he was sensible of it. The character of Hommais reveals a grudge against the scorners of the divine. But as soon as he turns toward religion, he finds nothing except what causes laughter and a shrugging of the shoulders. Account must be taken of his strange mania which leads straight to the cheapest literature of edification: "The man of the world at Mary's feet." "How a Christian servant should dress in warm weather." He discovers these naïve ecclesiastical little works as a pig finds truffles. He has the sadism of exasperation; he loves to be beside himself; it is his greatest pleasure. He will

repeat the same title in ten letters, the same sentence with
the same "enoooormous" which consoles him.

That observer who boasts of "representing," without his
personal feelings ever intervening in his work, carefully rejects
everything that does not contribute to comic effects, everything that does not make him cry out. Not that he did not encounter true mystics along his way. Let us recognize that he
holds them in horror. That man, who renounced wife, family,
profession and who lived in retirement at the river's edge, a
prisoner in a damp house, bent over a sentence for hours, considers the recluses of Port-Royal grotesque! "Why do you
find Schahabarim almost comical and your good men at Port-
Royal so serious?" he writes to Sainte-Beuve. "As for me, Monsieur Singlin is funereal alongside of my elephants. I look on
tattooed savages as being less anti-human, less plausible, less
laughable, less rare than people living in common, and calling
each other Monsieur until they die."

He went further in a letter to Michelet: "The great Voltaire ended the tiniest note by: *Ecr. l'inf.*[1] I have no authority
to say that word. From me to you, all encouragement would
be absurd, but I join you in hatred of the *anti-physis.*" L'anti-
physis! How easy it would be to connect with that imprudent
word all the letters in which Flaubert groans over his existence contrary to nature, and over the atrocious conditions to
which he submits! He has probably chosen them because he
prefers them and because nothing counts in his eyes but style;
but that does not prevent his knowing the enormity of his
life. Through his long correspondence runs the same moaning
and the old man repeats the complaint that the young recluse
of Croisset uttered: "It had given me pleasure to combat my
senses and to torture my heart. I refused the human intoxication offered me. Tooth and nail against myself, I uprooted the

---

[1] Ecrasez l'infâme. Down with the (Catholic) Church! Transl. note.

man with both hands, both hands full of strength and pride. From that tree with its green foliage, I wished to make a bare column so as to put some celestial flame way up there, as on an altar . . ."

It is Catholicism's perpetual requital to see constantly arising against her, in the name of Nature, those who violate her at every instant: all the prostitutions, all the victims of "strange and unfortunate errors," all those willingly poisoned. At least Flaubert's asceticism was purified of all that sullies and dishonors. He writes that he passes his days absolutely alone, with no more companion than if he were in the heart of Africa. This tragic disproportion between such renunciation and the idol that is its object, stifles him. He reads and rereads Spinoza to hearten himself, but the god of philosophers and scholars has no need for that holocaust; and Flaubert always ends by falling back on the human element.

Without his knowledge, all that remains for him is to look for the divine trail. His hatred of the bourgeois, that hatred instilled by Béranger, is born of the satisfaction that is displayed by beings of the golden mean over the comfort they find in getting along without God! "The dimensions of a soul can be measured by its suffering, as the depth of a river is measured by its current," he writes. The beaming bourgeois of the Agricultural show at d'Yonville irritate in him the dispossessed Christian from whom his Savior has been taken away. Only poets, philosophers and scholars seem logical beings to him; those who scrutinize reality, and those who represent it. He demands of them a total renunciation and a calm despair. He never admitted they had the right to settle down in life and Maxime du Camp loses his friendship as soon as he turns toward a good situation. The money that his young colleagues, a Zola or a Daudet, earned, made him a little jealous, perhaps, but shocked him especially. One must not be happy in the way of the world and an artist has no right to succeed.

It is true that Flaubert had always lived in the school of death. Death had, from his early childhood, prepared him for that detachment. The amphitheatre of the hospital at Rouen faced the garden where he played with his sister Caro: "How many times we climbed up the trellis and, hanging to the vines, looked curiously at the cadavers displayed there. The sun was shining overhead; the same flies that whirled over us and over the flowers went to alight there . . ."

So from childhood, Flaubert knew man's condition, and in spite of his anti-Catholicism, he takes a profound liking for the beings who search and for those who throw themselves into extremes: "The monks' robes with their knotted girdles arouse my soul in some ascetic and deep corners or other." That sentence is taken from a letter that contains admirable pages on prostitutes. In his opinion, one must know how to lose oneself: either in God, or in the lower regions. Only creators have the right to pull their boats up on the sand, but on the condition that they burn themselves out in work. If he admires Voltaire, it is because of his passion, his frenzy, and his great labor; but he hates Voltaire's followers: "People who laugh at great things," he says.

One can always laugh at great things and great men, and Flaubert, by the way, does not lack absurdity, if we have the heart to linger over it. The unusual conditions of his life make of him the blindest fellow for everything that does not touch on art and style. Not content with marrying his beloved niece to a Norman bourgeois of the type he has always the most looked down on, he sinks all his personal fortune into his nephew's business. The Bourgeois came to his enemy Flaubert and ruined him; on ruining him, he assassinated him, for

Flaubert died of the financial worries that kept him from working in peace.

Moreover, was the artist shrewder than his nephew? It does not seem as though he gave him good advice. That Flaubert of the last years of the Empire who strutted at Compiègne and at the Princess Mathilde's, writes as much foolishness as the most stupid of his contemporaries as soon as he meddles with politics. You must hear his oracles the year of Sadowa: "Well, in my opinion, I think the Emperor stronger than ever . . . The Emperor has Austria under his thumb, and in that question of foreign policy I find him strong beyond calculation whatever they may say." And he adds for his nephew: "If I were in business, I would go ahead jauntily now."

He does not see the storm coming, but he does see the approach of old age, inevitable torture. Age softens him mysteriously. He writes that he is getting soft with use. Old age has always obsessed him to the point that he formerly dreamed of writing a book on Sainte-Perrine. If we do not conceive of the end of life as a time of silence and meditation when everything abandons us purposely, when everything joins in leaving us alone in the presence of God still unseen, so that we may prepare to see Him face to face, how shall we pass our last days and nights? Sainte-Beuve, who is on the point of death, returns for a few months of life, and writes to Flaubert: " . . . A little note which reassures me as to his health," says Flaubert, "but very gloomy. He seems to be downcast at not being able to haunt the woods of Cypris . . ." Flaubert vainly adds that his friend is right after all "or at least right on his own way, which amounts to the same thing" . . . he can not keep from coming back to himself and trembles before the picture of a filthy old man . . . But

Gustave Flaubert will be protected from it by his very nature. He is not set up for enjoyment as he is for pain. His last letters are the most childishly tender. If he sometimes prowls around lingerie and the kitchen, it is not with the frightful face of the old Sainte-Beuve. "I satisfy my need for affection by calling Julie (his old servant) after my dinner, and I look at her black and white checked dress that mama wore. Then I dream of the good woman until tears choke me. Those are my pleasures . . ."

So in Flaubert, his heart must have endured to the end . . . that part of man which remains sensitive to God's touch. Did nothing of that kind happen? Was he not disturbed by any call? To tell the truth, it is not when he declares himself a Catholic that he seems to be closest to Christ. "As for me, I despise life; I am a Catholic . . ." Why no; it is, on the contrary, his hatred of life that keeps him from Catholicism, his contempt for man. To find the light, it would not have been enough for him to have safe-guarded the power of the heart, for he despised humanity, in himself and in others, to such a degree that he no longer perceived that part of the creature on which God puts his mark. It is not for nothing that at the end of his letters he couples terms of derision with his signature—and not only at the end of his letters. One day when Zola urged him to write a book on Morny and the Second Empire, Goncourt relates that Flaubert refused to do it, repeating that he was a *bedolle*. "A bedolle, what is that?" asked Daudet. "No one knows better than I how *bedolle* I am . . . Why, an old sheik!"—And Flaubert ended his sentence with a vaguely desperate gesture.

This elementary truth whose meaning the poor sheik has lost is that there exists in each one of us something that is not a subject for art and which is not meant to be exploited. Moreover, from the esthetic point of view, the soul could be expressed and represented only if it were not misunderstood. It is not that Flaubert was insensitive to that spiritual aspiration; but except in *Un Coeur Simple* and the character of Madame Arnoux, he makes us see it only aborted. For him, everything happens as though humanity, in search of the light, kept mistaking the door. The man who was able to write the *Three Tales* doubtless more than felt where life was, but he remained on the threshold. I am amazed that in his *Flaubert* Thibaudet compared Flaubert's esthetic Catholics with Baudelaire's Catholicism. Even if we did not have the exact testimony of *My Heart Laid Bare*, it is clear that for Baudelaire, even when he moans and cries out that he has no faith, the supernatural exists—the Christian supernatural—and that there remains, perhaps, in his eyes the unique reality without which the world of appearances would crumble and colors and forms would pass away.

Esthetic Catholicism, the expression is apt for Flaubert but not for the sinner, for the victim of the *Fleurs de Mal*. To be sure, esthetics could have opened to Flaubert that little door to the unknown Heaven through which Huysmans, his feeble disciple, entered the Church. We search certain texts in vain; at no time do we see Flaubert about to kneel. How could art, the final end of all his life, have become a means for him? This usurpation, this replacement of God by an idol seems irreparable to me on the supernatural plane (barring a miracle). God can always fill up an empty place in us; but what will He do if it is already entirely occupied, if it is deliberately and jealously reserved for Mammon or Venus, Apollo and the Muses?

To be sure, we find other reasons for Flaubert's refusal outside of him: first his epoch, as we have already remarked; the atmosphere of that century drawing to a close when the great were not satisfied to deny Christianity, for they had

organized its funeral; they had drawn up the account of its
death duties. Renan made the inventory after the death of
the Christian God in the name of the divinity who had assassinated Him in order to succeed Him: Science. It would
doubtless have been necessary for that Flaubert whom we have
seen so devoid of political acumen, so servile to pontiffs with
a prestige equal to that of Sainte-Beuve, Michelet, Renan and
Berthelot. But he associated with hardly anyone except the
old Didon, his niece Caroline's friend. The famous Dominican's letters to Madame Commanville have just been published; the man inspires sympathy, and his sufferings during
his exile in Corsica are touching. But what a gay bird, attracted by all the mirrors of fashion! Dazzled by the enemy,
persuaded they are the advocates of a lost cause, trustees of
an infinite richness of which they are not clearly enough conscious, thus the men often appear who might have been able
to open a Flaubert's eyes! "Madame Bovary is myself . . ."
he said. But perhaps Emma never resembles him more than
when, turning eagerly toward the curate Bournisien, she runs
up against a gloomy being, incapable of understanding her,
and who, with his eyes closed, disgorges formulas learned by
heart. In many of Flaubert's letters, we perceive signs of disillusionment and disappointed hope. As early as 1846, at the
baptism of his little Caroline, he is aware of that frightful
bungling of the liturgy: "The priest mumbled as fast as he
could a Latin he couldn't hear . . . The most intelligent of
all were certainly the stones that had formerly understood all
that, and which, perhaps, had retained some of it." So he
recognized that something goes on living beyond formulas
and gestures.

But probably Flaubert would have been changed in no way
had he encountered a saint along his way. He would have
taken the stage-coach of Ars-en-Dombes in vain; the deform-

ing glass through which he looked at man and the world would, in his eyes, have contorted the face of the curate of Ars, as the rest of creation. And he probably possessed some of the virtues God demands of those He has chosen: hatred of the world, a liking for solitude, of renunciation, detachment, perseverance, a certainty that the kingdom of art belongs to the violent. Perhaps he lacks the essential: charity in its deepest sense. Perfect toward his friends, family and servants, to be sure, we have seen that Flaubert despised the creature none the less. During the war and after the Commune, his reflexes of a "novelist disturbed in his habits" are savage. All the mandarins of the Magny dinner have hardly one heart. But Flaubert is the most guilty of all, he, so evidently made for love and whose source of tenderness appeared intact to the very end. He shoved it aside deliberately. When Goncourt asserts: "Neither Flaubert, nor Zola nor I have ever been seriously in love and we are incapable of depicting love . . ." he is grossly deceived as far as Flaubert is concerned; but the truth is there never was a man who exerted more perseverance in hardening himself. What he accomplished is, in the words of Charles Du Bos "A transfer of the heart to the head." And Du Bos adds: "What Flaubert asks of his personal life is the beating itself of continuity, the exclusion of the accidental, the monotony of a long and heavy task of the heat given off by its gradual accomplishment." And he hates others with an often unworthy hatred, all the others who break that continuity. He grumbles at the poor who knock at his door at Croisset during a long hard winter.

The whole question is one of knowing whether man has the right to cut himself off from the world and to mutilate himself, when it is not with a view to the kingdom of God. To be sure, nothing disturbs a life more than love, and the highest love upsets it more than any other. Before that long front

that extends from the creature to the Creator and which tries
to invest the loving and weak heart of a man, the artist closes
up, bristles and rolls himself into a ball. If only a man, God
and the Man-God himself would let the man of letters work in
peace! But the eunuch sometimes can not bear himself and
feels his ugliness; so the writer, the "inky beast," hates himself and hates his neighbor as himself; he intoxicates himself
with scorn. An entomologist does not dislike insects, but the
novelist naturally loathes the human beast. To be sure, Flaubert did not give in entirely to that baseness; he kept himself
from it even in his most bitter books. (I am thinking of
Justin, of the little clerk Hommais on the evening of Emma's
burial: "Over the grave, between the evergreens, a child was
weeping on her knees, and her breast, torn by sobs, was rising
and falling in the shadow . . .") It is less in Flaubert's work
than in that of his miserable children that this hatred of man
oozes out: in a Zola or a Huysmans. Still the latter, by observing human grimaces, ended by noticing a resemblance:
the absurd face became, little by little, pitiful, then noble,
then sacred. "It is necessary to make life and truth through
the beautiful, just the same." That is what Flaubert wanted
and what he did not get, perhaps. Was it his finical attachment to form that prevented him from "making live"? No, if
life does not tremble in his work as in that of a Dostoyefsky
or an Eliot, the writer's scruples must not be blamed for it.
Doubtless, the anxiety he often betrayed in his letters by
this expression "I am going to sit myself down to sentences"
. . . helps us understand how dangerous such a work is for
the direct expression of a still warm reality. On the other
hand, this disadvantage is amply balanced by the composi-
tion of Flaubertian pictures, those symphonies in which, by
means of art, complex reality is given back to us, and sometimes vibrates as strongly as in any other work spontaneously

sprung into being. But it is rare, very rare when Flaubert does not remain a little to one side of life. We remain outside of the drama he is relating to us. If we never feel pulled along or rolled over by the flow of the novel, if we watch it flow from the banks, we must not look for reasons of an esthetic nature; it is not because the author "sits down to sentences," takes a long time to choose epithets, exercises his mind with assonances. It is on the spiritual plane that the weakness of this art appears to us.

Eliot, Tolstoi, Dostoyefsky, each in his own way, gives us the impression of touching the bottom of the being. Flaubert, even if he had not had that obsessing preoccupation with style, would not have gone further into man. We come back to this truth that it is a great weakness for a novelist to put the infinite into the ridiculous. We have all known, in our bourgeois families, certain of our kin who would have made Flaubert wild-eyed with joyous exasperation. And yet, under that comedy mask, often a drama is being played that Flaubert would not even have suspected. We know the absurdities of Hommais and Bournisien; we are not sure of knowing Bournisien and Hommais. To be sure, it is possible there is nothing behind those laughable and immortal faces, but perhaps, too, they are concealing a world, the one that Dostoyefsky would have attained without effort.

Almost all Flaubert's creatures express themselves in clichés. Flaubert was always struck by the fact that most people repeat ready-made sentences and exchange indefinitely a small number of ideas accepted (of which, in his youth, he amused himself by making up the catalogue) . So the problem for him consists in not being caught in that net-work of conventional words, but in reaching, through it, in his characters, that part of them they do not express. Those banal remarks and conventional language must allow the real depths to show through, as happens in the case of Madame Bovary. If all too often that appearance seems to hide no reality, it is because Flaubert himself did not believe in that reality. This fanatic in art betrayed art since he cut it off at the roots. One essential work should preside at all the creations of a man, and that is his own life. A life purified and holy, that is the work of works that sometimes flowers the cells of a San Marco, inspires the Divine Comedy, makes Pascal set down, on the first sheet of paper that comes to his hand, his thoughts still living and warm;—and even those whose vocation it is to bring the creature to life in imaginary tales, benefit by Christian deprivation; we know well only that of which we are deprived. To be sure it happens that the passion which burns, drags from man some fine outbursts; but how get acquainted with it while one is undergoing it? How could we heat up that fire with a look, assign it its true place, if we are fighting in the midst of flames, if we are stifling under the debris?

Yet it is not enough to escape the fire. No masterpiece is created without love. Flaubert repudiates his youth and enters a cell; properly speaking, nothing belongs to him any more except his disillusionment and his bitterness. That does not prevent him from being nauseated by the naturalism coming out of him. That father did not want such a monster to be his child, and he persuaded himself that the contempt for style which Zola affected disgraced his works. But the great Flaubert's style, at the end of his life, masks the same poverty. It seems as though, in the portrait of Madame Arnoux and in the *Three Tales*, he spent all the youth and love he had in him, in spite of himself. Now nothing is left for him but to die of a laborious and dismal farce, and to incarnate himself in two half-wits that his genius has made immortal.

LOTI

D URING A LONG WINTER STUDY IN THE FOURTH GRADE, I opened *Sailor* which a friend had given me. I recall that distress in which the monitor caught me, that inability to tear myself away from the powerful enchantment. I never wanted to open the revealing work again; I have retained none of it except the vision of a youth who, before embarking, goes at dawn to say goodbye to that estate near the village where he had been a child; the garden-gate receives his face held out to it. I remember, too, a pontoon where a mother waits in the rain; she is dressed up to receive the son who is not to come back . . . So Loti, during a long winter study, was already spreading out the shadow of death over my boyhood. Nothing is so brief, I said to myself, as that youth, in appearance so boundless.

What is that secret impossibility in love? Do we feel it only by the wrench of long separations? The sea, unknown lands, strange and passing loves, all that helps us wait for death. Under other skies, we forget the foul, Western agitation, and if the Orient is closed to us, there remain old regions in France which the Atlantic cradles and puts to sleep, sequestered races, mysterious and forbidden.

What poet of the last century and of our own has not developed that theme? The eternal passing of things, the great river of forgetfulness that rolls us toward the nameless pit;

for a century, all our literature has exhausted itself with that motif. But the others claimed to establish a system; they had general ideas and liked to reason; intellectual byplay was amusing to them. But for forty years, Loti never stopped howling at death. All his work is only a monotonous, heart-breaking complaint. Listen to that child in the shadows; you can not reassure him because he does not understand your reasoning. He gathers up and desperately broods over the vestiges of his loves; he blows on the cold cinders, clutters up his memory and his house with relics, clutches at all the branches along the banks fleeing past, and never lets go of the dead leaves which he holds in his hands.

Does that state of fright, that distress in which it is Pascal's intention to keep us, at least have some spiritual benefit? Christ has come to offer an inconceivable challenge to the apparent passing of things: "I will draw all things unto me." Everything, poor Loti; and even that evening, on the Gulf of Salonika where Aziyadé's bark cleft the black water; every-thing, even that autumn road where Ramuncho's sandals made their silent march; everything, even the shadows of that cell where you loosened your brother Yves' chains . . . To be sure Loti was sensitive to the humanity of Christ. If he had encountered Him along his way, living and mortal, doubtless he would have followed Him; but he would only have followed Him until he was put into the tomb. Do not ask him to adhere to a metaphysics. He makes all manner of fun of your reason-ing. Nothing exists for him that the hands and lips do not touch. Islamism that materializes Christianity, fits him; that is why he cherished it so. He would doubtless have embraced it if the impossibility of believing anything had not been his only share in the Western inheritance. Did not those who have read the burning confessions of Isabelle Eberhardt dream that in that nomadic child, a prey to the desert and

unhappy love, flesh submissive to the will of Allah, the destiny
of Loti was being worked out?

Of the countries and skies that this sailor opens to our
dreams, there is one that one never thinks to recall was the
real Columbus. Others before him had dragged us over all
the oceans and rivers. But only Loti lighted up for us the
dark places in those savage hearts. Yves, Ramuncho, spahis,
quartermasters, fishermen, wild birds and great albatrosses
that he captured and held for a few moments. Loti certainly
had the right to detest naturalism as he did; the work of a
Zola or a Maupassant misrepresents the peasant and the
worker. He alone, through vulgarities and surface brutalities,
has reached that virgin soul of the people, that unknown land
whose eternal aspect no culture has changed, that sea which,
in spite of the worst violence, has its secret charm, its real
goodness and its long fidelities.

But if he pitied their miserable lives, that subjection to
blind discipline, that agony in the bush, or on a hospital cot,
or in glacial oceans, if he showed us, on roads and break-
waters, desperate mothers and wives who wait no more, Loti
never knew the temptation of breathing revolt or construct-
ing systems. He was cured of all hope; nothing prevails,
thinks he, against pain or death of which everything called
progress has only known how to strengthen the rule. Then
rock yourselves to sleep, sailors, with old songs, taste the destruction of deadly alcohols and tight embraces; console your
hearts in black and gold churches; everything is good that
appeases and puts to sleep.

Why would young men, ambitious to understand and to
act, not withdraw from such a work? Born of the sea, it has
its uniformity, monotony and overwhelming murmuring.

Nothing to base on that sand that the tides wear away; and they remember a remark of Vauvenargues: "The thought of death deceives us, for it makes us forget to live." But what is it to live? Where is the true life? There is not a builder or fighter who does not give in sometimes and feel painfully the vanity of his effort; secret despair to think that at Babylon and Carthage, soldiers died for a country they were told was eternal . . . And the world will perish too . . . No, the thought of death did not deceive the Christ, nor all the martyrs, nor a Blaise Pascal. It can become a source of life. It was Loti's misfortune that he saw in it, not a point of departure, not a means, but an end. He did not pass beyond it, because he was satisfied here. Pain must be loved as a penitence and as a bond of union between us and Christ; Loti cherished it voluptuously. Sometimes he seemed to admit its power of redemption and salvation, but he claimed also to arm himself with a grudge against the unknown God. The torments of his heart were to him so sovereign a good that he did not want Joy.

BARRÈS

I F, SINCE HE HAS LEFT US, MAURICE BARRÈS IS IGNORANT OF
the silence and the lack of interest which hardly ever
spares the most illustrious man the day after his death, it is
probably because, when the great oak has been cut down, we
measure its stature by the space of earth and sky suddenly
uncovered, better than when it was alive and standing.

But shall we say it is to the memory of Barrès that we remain faithful? We do not have to recall a master who has not
left us. He remains among his sons; he disturbs them, stimu-
lates and sometimes irritates them; death has not interrupted
the dialogue between Barrès and those who have been born
of him. The passionate debate goes on which that father opposed to his numerous children—or rather that big brother to
his restless young brothers.

What debate? In the young Barrès of *Under the Eyes
of the Barbarians* and *The Enemy of the Laws*, the most
furious and desperate of the newly arrived can recognize
themselves—and those, too, who grant no significance to the
word "truth," who have lost faith in intelligence and, in
hatred of all discipline, submit themselves to what is darkest
in them and cultivate their confusion and their inner chaos.
They all resemble that twenty-year-old Barrès, ardent and
discouraged at the same time. A meeting ground that, moreover, has nothing remarkable about it; there is considerable

artifice in the oppositions that men try to create between the generation of defeat, that of the eighties, that of the type "Agathon," the post-war one. Difference of circumstances only. According to the epoch, we can attribute that eternal restlessness which goes on, from generation to generation, to the shame of having been defeated or the disappointments of victory; to tell the truth, it is the attribute of all youth; it is born of the first look that man, while scarcely out of childhood, casts upon his heart and the world.

Just as brothers who do not look like each other, resemble their common father, so there are hardly any young writers to-day who can not find themselves again in the rebel of *Under the Eyes of the Barbarians;* but there is hardly a one, too, who has consented to look for salvation as Barrès wished, from the *Garden of Bérénice* on. Here we are touching on a profound disagreement between Barrès and many of his spiritual sons. Nothing throws more light on this disagreement than the inquest on politics conducted, so many years ago now, by the *Revue hebdomadaire,* among writers of thirty or forty years of age; a regrettable inquest in which was betrayed an almost general indifference to political affairs. With what a shrugging of the shoulders Barrès would have received it! As a boy he had claimed to think it stupid for one to be able to believe that anything of importance exists in the world; but soon that to which he denied importance, if not interest and charm, was the individual and ephemeral; he withdraws from everything that does not endure, in order to adhere passionately to what does endure, to what is eternal, or at least to what has some chance of endurance and eternity: to France.

"What can young Frenchmen find of greater interest than the problems of the Rhine?" Barrès asks in the *Genius of the Rhine*. The writers do not represent a whole generation, thank heavens; but it is serious, just the same, when we neglect to serve the great cause for which Barrès lived.

Yet his example shows us that this service does not demand total renunciation of meditation or dreaming. A Barrès was not enclosed in his nationalist doctrine as in a blockhouse. We know that he feared above everything closed systems where others live walled in. After the *Garden on the Orontes* he reserved many other airs for us. It was only a game for that Ariel to escape organized forces and to attain that shady realm which he liked. On the first pages of the last book he signed for us: *An Inquest into the Countries of the Levant,* he helps us understand the rhythm of his life, divided between the necessities of national service and the deepest poetry: "To-day, the day after an electoral campaign, to reward myself, I am going to pass over the zone of clear countries and penetrate into the mysterious circle. I shall give myself a brilliant vision, I shall awaken within me new songs and I shall harmonize myself with moving facts that I feel but do not know. I need to hear deeper and more mysterious music and to rejoin my dreams that I have placed on the other side of the sea, at the entrance to the desert of Asia. It is a question of giving pleasure to myself some day after so much constraint."

Probably, if none of us seems to retain that agility for changing the atmosphere, if it is given to none of Barrès' successors to spend the afternoon in the tribune of the Chamber, or in the bosom of Commissions, to find once more in his heart, that same evening "that Asiatic land all rustling with dreams of unorganized forces," it is probably a lack of genius and poverty in the specialist. It was hard for Barrès to conceive of literature as occupying the whole life of a man; and he felt some scorn for the men of letters who are only that. Yet, several of them (and I am thinking especially of the

novelists) , can find an excuse when the memory of their master torments them: literature is not, for them, only a recipe
for charming and moving themselves, nor a music to set them
free. Far from wishing to escape the barbarians, it has become
almost impossible for them to turn aside, be it ever so little,
from their vocation, which is the knowledge of man. Secrets
of the heart obsess them to the point that most of them seem
to have lost the sense of indignation and distaste, nothing
makes them indignant, nothing human disgusts them. That
passion to let nothing essential escape, in them or in others,
helps us understand, without excusing them, that the writers
of to-day approach subjects formerly forbidden, free themselves and reveal their secret wounds with a desperate sincerity.

But we doubt that this effort, perhaps vain, to advance in
the knowledge of man, is compatible with a life consumed by
politics. On the evening of a day in parliament, and after so
many hours lived in the thick of men, Barrès is able to charm
himself by relating to himself *A Garden on the Orontes*. But
if it is to man that his mind continues to attach itself, will he
be able suddenly to forget his preferences and his hatred of
parties? It will be those generous hatreds, on the contrary
which will serve him best on that plane. *Their Faces* is doubtless an eternal book; yet if we admire that savage painting, it
disappoints us too in proportion as it is that very knowledge
of man that is important to us, and not his grimaces, however
pathetic. Here we do not claim to approve the political indifference of many of to-day's writers—only to find an excuse
for them; it is not granted many to solve the paradox which
Barrès conquered: Barrès (may Montherlant pardon me!)
at the same time a great writer and a great Frenchman.

In this generation, when literary talent abounds, there is no
one who retains Barrès' power to change his star, to pass from

art to politics and to make one serve the other. But even set-
ting politics aside, do many exist who still believe a writer can
serve? Of which one of us can we hope for a page which would
be for the youth of to-day what the admirable preface to the
Disciple was to those of 1889? Neither Bourget nor Barrès
has left to our generation a sense of responsibility.

Or perhaps we feel ourselves responsible for a more humble
task, but one that only we can fulfill. Barrès liked to quote the
remark of Novalis: "Chaos must gleam through the regular
veil of order." It is no longer a question of us watching this
confused world gleam in order to extract enjoyment from it,
nor even of discovering in it fine musical themes; nor of veil-
ing it, nor arranging it according to an outer rule, but of
knowing it as it is. We try to persuade ourselves that it is
serving France to maintain her in the first ranks of the nations
who know man best—to whom no conflicts of the human
being are unknown.

Would Barrès have condemned us? I recall him at the
burial of Marcel Proust of whom he had been very fond without recognizing his greatness. I believe that at that time, he
was beginning to perceive it. But let us not doubt it: one
defect in that work, and one that could be found in many
other works of to-day, would always have discouraged him:
is that he would have found nothing in it which could serve
what he considered the only necessity: the education of the
soul.

II

The Judges of Barrès

Maurice Barrès has no luck for the twenty-fifth anniversary
of his death (1949); his judges belong to a generation the
least capable of liking him, that goes without saying, why

even of trying to understand him. I should like to indicate here why I take exception to the various literary juries which, to-day, allow themselves to condemn or absolve him.

First, let us agree that never have historical combinations of events weighed more heavily on Letters. All the Sister Annes of criticism, caught between the existentialist feed and the feed of absurdity, who question the horizon and worry because they do not see anyone coming, forget that a time like ours belongs to the whole of history. A people does not come out of the greatest defeat it has ever undergone nor of an enemy occupation of four years without the bookstore being given over to the defeated generals, to all the unhappy ministers, and the Machiavellis who, under the impression they were only clever, refuse to look like traitors, without counting the actors in good faith, persuaded that they were serving France, and who perhaps in fact did serve her, but would like to prove it to themselves and others. These cheap writers of memoirs flood the bookstore windows and yield to the illusion that they will be able to touch up their eternal image, fixed forever in History. And I am not counting the victims who recount their martyrdom, or the witnesses skillful in benefiting themselves by the importance of the events in which they have taken part, and authors of "war diaries" in which it often happens that their own emptiness, on the contrary, bursts forth, and forces itself on us with a lugubrious evidence. And I was going to forget Marx whom those who had read him explain and comment on in a hundred volumes for the rest of humanity that wants to be revolutionized by *Capital*, but on condition that they never poke their noses into it.

During this period when a vanquished country examines its conscience and looks for the reasons of its misfortunes, it is inevitable that literary creation suffer from it. Since the scene remains almost empty, it is also inevitable that professors of philosophy should invade and occupy it. Among those professors, those conquer who, gifted in dialectics, excel in illustrating, by concrete examples, the system, generally borrowed, to which they attach their names. So Paul Bourget, formerly, a sociologist lost in novels, told stories in the style of Bonald and Le Play. On the literary plane, and leaving out of the question, to be sure, the "thinker" and the dialectician, Sartre would be a little our Bourget; at any rate, he has nothing in common with Barrès, Chateaubriand's descendant; he has no place in that royal line of which Montherlant and Malraux are the last links; he does not belong to the family. The philosopher Lagneau reproached Barrès one day "for having stolen the instrument." Philosophy avenged itself; it could be said she has paid us back, and with what talent? And what brilliance! That does not prevent the literary instrument, in the hands of the most brilliant philosophers, from finally turning against literature.

For these philosophers act, they are virulent, they attack the French tree at its roots. A philosopher who denies there is anything permanent in man, who teaches that man is only what he does, what poison for the descendants of Pascal, La Rochefoucauld, La Bruyère and Joubert! It contradicts that truth, mother of all literatures, source of all the great works of the novel and theatre, the *Oedipus*, of *Hamlet* and of *Phèdre* "traitorous and incestuous in spite of oneself," that we do not resemble certain of our acts and that many of our acts do not resemble us. We are that part of ourselves which has a horror of our shortcomings and our crimes, and we are also that base part of ourselves which now yields to greed and now submits itself to what the Christian calls Grace; but what does the name matter? Phèdre was, all the same, different from her life; she was not her life. When this secret is once lost, a literature finds itself nearing its end.

The objection will be raised: "It is you who say so, but great works are already expressing, under an empty sky, that soulless man who has nothing except his life." Where are those works? I see that our literature is getting lost on the dead-end road of erotism and abjection which leads nowhere except to inarticulate cries of folly. Here, surrealism enters into the play of the philosophers, although they detest themselves. Commentaries with crazy barkings can be read in serious critical reviews. As Joseph de Maistre dares to write: "God would laugh if He could laugh." So let Barrès take exception to those who pass judgment on him to-day, and let him come back in twenty-five years! But in 1973, will there be a single heart or thought to welcome his dear Shadow? Will pious hands be found to brush aside the thick grass of forgetfulness on that stone where the greatest names fade?

A BRIEF CASE
FOR ANDRÉ GIDE

PROBABLY THE GOOD SHEEP-DOGS, CLAUDEL AND JAMMES, growl and turn about this lost sheep who carries the taste for conversion to the point of being converted to a different truth every day. Nevertheless, let us try to understand, in Gide, a case of terrible sincerity. There is not a sign in him of what Stendhal unjustly calls hypocrisy and which he denounces in the men of the seventeenth century. It is true that the choice of a doctrine obliges us, at times when the forces within us deny it, to continue to profess with our lips until the return of Grace. Gide is a man who would not resign himself to inclining the automat even for a moment.

What a compliment in that reproach that he wished to express only his youth ". . . without worrying about expressing anything else, and wishing only to express it better . . ." Let us grant to that love of perfection and scrupulousness a value even moral. Any one of Gide's books is for us a lesson in moderation and renunciation—formal renunciation but one that includes also the heart. Let us learn from him the refusal of easy success, and that dignity of the writer which is an eminent virtue. Which of our elders will teach us contempt for passing fame?

It means nothing to say that Gide does not choose. He chooses to think, but thought is action; he chooses to taste,

117

but taste is active. A Gide is of all the more service because he does not premeditate service. He serves France by writing better French than anyone else. Subjected to a moral aim, his language would, perhaps, be less pure. That exquisite art is of value because of its gratuitousness. At any rate, put to practical ends, it would be something else. It is not a question of holding him up as a model; everyone has his mission, and I agree there should not be many Gides in Letters . . . but I don't think there is any danger . . .

What is called the "antagonism between esthetics and morality" gives its human value to Gide's work. Catholic creators here recognize the great debate which tears them apart (I say creators, not critics). If, when converted, it is finally granted us to end that debate, should we insult our less fortunate masters and comrades? Outside of Catholicism, Gide's attitude offers nothing shocking to the reason. His inner confusion becomes, without doubt, the subject matter of his art; but that is the highest use a Godless man can make of his poverty.

By denouncing Gide's taste for "feline natures," and for primitive and savage beings, one obtains an easy effect in court. Why omit to recall that this taste is common to all artists? It partly explains Stendhal's work, and Mérimée's. The one in Italy, the other in Spain and Corsica did nothing but look for Lafcadios, beings who make their own laws. It never seemed to me, unless one were Catholic, that one could love any one of the people for any other quality than that new force, that stream that nothing has yet dammed up.

An ancient practice of Catholicism helps us penetrate Gide's secret. He must have been one of those children of whom it is said in Christian families: he has a vocation. For this man, so wavering, was always the prey to a fixed idea: to act on young hearts. Let us recognize by that sign a man predestined to apostleship; but, born out of the fold, what could he do with that fearful gift? Will it not become, for him, "an end in itself"? That does not prevent his work from bearing testimony. It reveals to us only disappointed joys, irritated thirsts, vain experiences, and that silence of the aged Narcissus leaning over the fountain, and suddenly turning away, his eyes full of tears. Because it irritates our thirst, it makes us remember the water of Jacob's well.

Multiple, Gide frees himself in his works. It is not his living disciples but the sons of his genius whom he enjoins to make the dangerous or forbidden gestures. Lafcadio can do evil; he can do good too; for every poison kills or cures according to the dose, and according to the disposition that receives it. What writer would boast of troubling no one? Who knows if certain "judgments" will not disgust certain Catholic minds forever?

On the one hand, the author of *The Immoralist* and *The Strait Gate* is what mystics call an introvert to the point that nothing, in his holy friend, the lieutenant Dupouey, disconcerts him. He has made us acquainted with the noblest and the vilest hearts. But every man who enlightens us on ourselves prepares the way of Grace within us. Gide's mission is to throw the torches over the cliffs and to collaborate in our examination of conscience. Let us not follow him further; he himself begs us not to follow him, and to forearm ourselves against all the masters who are not the Master. Gide demoniacal? Ah! less, probably, than many a right-thinking writer who exploits the immense herd of readers, and especially the "guided" feminine readers; and not more than Socrates, accused of corrupting the youth, because it learned from him to know itself. I remember one evening having heard Gide defend the Christ with a strange passion; let us await God's judgment.

RADIGUET

W AS RAYMOND RADIGUET AN INFANT PRODIGY? HE WAS, at any rate, prodigiously lucid, a lucidity without equal at so early an age. Those of us who were imprudent enough to publish books at twenty, have later recognized how their first youth deformed the world and themselves. Not any more than a dead man has come back to describe to us what was going on beyond the tomb, has any boy before Radiguet revealed to us the secret of his youth; we were reduced to our memories which are touched-up photographs. His work owes its shocking appearance to this lack of retouching, because nothing resembles cynicism more than clairvoyance.

So *The Devil in the Body* shocked, and it also upsets the numerous race of those who do not like rising suns. But, they told themselves, in order to take heart again, the property of a miracle lies in its not renewing itself; and here is a boy who is emptying his school-bag before us; his experience is too short for him to find much to say to us . . . Alas! On December 12, 1923, they could add "Raymond Radiguet will not tell us anything more." . . .

Yet, here is *Count d'Orgel's Ball*. Did Radiguet know in advance he should not lose any time? It was enough for him to pass through the world without saying anything, to pick up that splendid booty. Being in a hurry, he did not take the trouble to disguise the face of his models; and *Count d'Orgel's*

Ball will give those who enjoy the game of removing masks amusement in so doing; but let them not stop there. There is no book which deserves less than that one to be called a novel of real persons, or which attains more surely the universal.

To write *Count d'Orgel's Ball* at the age of twenty, it is not enough to be generously endowed with the rarest gifts; one must have reflected over his trade; and it is praiseworthy that, while still so young, Radiguet knew how to bring out the two laws of the novel, essential, according to us . . . "a novel in which it is the psychology that is romantic," he himself wrote regarding the *Ball*; "the whole effort of the imagination is applied there, not to external happenings, but to the analysis of feelings." Does the psychological novel differ from the novel of adventure? "In nothing; it is the same thing," answers Radiguet, and he proves it. *Count d'Orgel's Ball* offers more vicissitudes and keeps us more breathless than any book full of intrigues, yet everything goes on inside the beings. What is called a novel of adventure, which is only an artificial entangling of circumstances, can indeed divert us, in the Pascalian sense of the word, that is, turn us away from ourselves. However, it is within ourselves that our adventure, the only drama that interests us is being played, and it is for the true artist to lead us to it. I would swear that of all his works, Monsieur Pierre Benoît looks upon his *Mademoiselle de la Ferté* with the most favor.

As for the second law whose acquaintance permits a boy to write that masterpiece of stature, *Count d'Orgel's Ball*, Radiguet's age and the conditions of his life would, it seems, have rendered its discovery singularly difficult. He said of his book: "A chaste novel of love, as improper as the most impure novel . . ." To evaluate justly such a discovery, we must remember the apparent disorder in which that brief life burnt itself out. Discipline was not the order of the day in the society in which Radiguet moved. Listen how Jean Cocteau relates the "apparition" of that strange child nourished on the extreme left of letters, and who, more than any one of us, deserves the epithet of classic.

". . . Raymond Radiguet appeared. He was fifteen and claimed to be eighteen, which confuses his biographers. He never had his hair cut. He was near-sighted, almost blind and rarely opened his mouth. The first time he came to see me, sent by Max Jacob, I was told: 'In the waiting-room, there is a child with a cane . . .' As he lived at Saint-Maur Park, along the Marne, we called him the miracle of the Marne. He seldom went home, slept anywhere at all, on the ground, on tables, with the painters of Montparnasse and Montmartre. Sometimes he pulled out of his pocket a dirty little torn piece of paper. The scrap was passed around and they read a poem as fresh as a seashell or a bunch of currants."

Not only did Radiguet live in that anarchy, but he saw the success too of the newly arrived in Letters, almost all busy in depicting men and women whose sole vocation was pleasure. Anyone else would have entrusted himself to Morand's furrow, and, without doubt, would have been lost in it. Nothing, in our opinion, demonstrates better the extraordinary merit of Morand than the interest he forces us to take in creatures so stripped as his, and in whom passion runs up against nothing. In Morand, no possible conflict; and besides we don't even think of it, dazzled by pictures, intoxicated by odors, bathed in an atmosphere that satisfies our joy. With erotism lying in wait, in which so many young talented men of to-day have come to flounder, Paul Morand walks along the cliff and avoids falling in. Radiguet, too, does not even permit it to approach. If he had the devil in his body, look how austere the principles of his art were.

"Atmosphere useful for the unfolding of certain sentiments," he writes in the margin of *The Ball*, "but it is not a painting of the world." It is because he could permit himself the luxury of scorning the scenery; he shows us souls.

In Mahaut d'Orgel, Radiguet's heroine, purity of heart gives importance to love. Her conjugal tenderness and her ignorance of passion prevent her from recognizing the delightful invasion of it. Her purity even drags her down dangerous steps. The richer our moral life is, the more complicated our sentiments, and the more their interpretation demands of both simplicity and subtility. Radiguet shows us, through glass, the workings of hearts entirely engaged in deceiving themselves. "This is what they think they are discovering in themselves. This is what is really going on," he seems to tell us. All his art as a novelist is based on that formula. Perhaps he is too much the master of his creatures; they never drag him along; they follow in a straight line, from which we sometimes wish they would deviate; one would say it was a spring that is extended in accordance with wise foresight . . . but it is the attribute of a passion that leads everything to itself, to regulate all our acts with an aim to satisfying them; passion, to a certain degree, mechanizes us. That is what was very well seen by Radiguet who would quickly have acquired more suppleness. Such as it is, his work is enough for us, his elders; the cause is clear, that child was a master.

GRAHAM GREENE

T HE WORK OF AN ENGLISH CATHOLIC NOVELIST—OF AN
Englishman returning to Catholicism—like *The Power
and the Glory* by Graham Greene, at first always gives me the
sensation of being in a foreign land. To be sure, I find there
my spiritual country, and it is into the heart of a familiar
mystery that Graham Greene introduces me. But everything
takes place as though I were penetrating into an old estate
through a concealed door unknown to me, hidden in a wall
covered with ivy, and as though I were advancing behind the
hero of a novel through tangled branches and suddenly recognized the great avenue of the park where I played when I
was a child and deciphered my initials cut on the trunk of
an oak on some former holiday.

A French Catholic enters the church by the main door
only; he is interwoven with its official history; he has taken
part in all the debates which have torn it throughout the
centuries and which have divided the Gallican church especially. In everything he writes, one discovers at once whether
he is on the side of Port-Royal or the Jesuits, whether he
weds Bossuet's quarrel with Fénélon, whether he is on the
side of Lamennais and Lacordaire or if it is with Louis
Veuillot that he agrees. Bernanos' work of which it is impossible not to think on reading *The Power and the Glory* is
very significant in this respect. All the Catholic controversies

of the last four centuries unfold in filigree. Behind the Abbé
Donissan of the *Sun of Satan*, appears the curate of Ars.
Bernanos' saints, like his liberal priests and like the pious laymen he describes with such happy ferocity, betray his venera-
tions and his hatreds.

Graham Greene, himself, broke, like a burglar, into the
kingdom of the unknown, into the kingdom of nature and of
Grace. No prejudice troubles his vision. No current of ideas
turns him aside from that discovery, that key which he found
suddenly. He has no preconceived notion of what we call a
bad priest; it could be said that he has no model of saintliness
in his mind. There is corrupted nature and omnipotent
Grace; there is poverty-stricken man who is nothing, even in
evil, and there is mysterious love which lays hold upon him
in the thick of his ridiculous misery and absurd shame to
make a saint and martyr of him.

The power and the glory of the Father burst forth in the
Mexican curate who loves alcohol too much and who gets
one of his parishioners pregnant. A type so common and
mediocre that his mortal sins call forth only derision and a
shrugging of the shoulders, and he knows it. What this extraordinary book shows us is, if I dare say so, the utilization
of sin by Grace. This priest, rebellious and condemned to
death by the public authorities and on whose head there is a
price (the drama takes place in a Mexico given over to atheistic and persecuting rulers), who tries to save himself, as
indeed all the other priests, even the most virtuous, did, who
in fact saves himself and passes the frontier, but who comes
back every time a dying person needs him, even when he believes his help will be in vain, and even when he is not
ignorant that it is a trap and that the one who is calling him
has already betrayed him, this priest, a drunkard, impure
and trembling before death, gives his life without for a single

moment losing the feeling of his baseness and his shame. He would think it a joke if he were told he was a saint. He is miraculously saved from pride, complacency and self-righteousness. He goes to his martyrdom, having always in his mind the vision of the soiled nothingness and the sacrilege that a priest in a state of mortal sin is, so that he sacrifices himself on attributing to God all of that power and glory which triumph over what he considers the most miserable of men: himself.

And as he approaches the end, we see this mediocre sinner conform slowly to the Christ until he resembles Him, but that is not saying enough: until he identifies himself with his Lord and his God. Passion begins again around this victim chosen from among human derelicts, who repeats what Christ did, not as at the altar, without it costing him anything, on offering the blood and the body under the species of bread and wine, but giving up his own flesh and blood as on a cross. In this false, bad priest it is not virtue that appears as the opposite of sin, it is faith—faith in that sign he received the day of his ordination, in the trust that he alone (since all the other priests have been massacred or have fled) still bears in his hands, unworthy but yet consecrated.

The last priest remaining in the country, he is unable not to believe that after him there will be no one to offer the Sacrifice, or to absolve, or to distribute the bread which is no longer bread, or to help the dying on the threshold of life eternal. And yet his faith does not waver, although he does not know that scarcely will he have fallen when another priest will suddenly and furtively appear.

We feel it is that hidden presence of God in an atheistic world, that subterranean flowing of Grace which dazzles Graham Greene much more than the majestic façade which the temporal Church still erects above the peoples. If there is a Christian whom the crumbling of the invisible Church would not disturb, it is, indeed, that Graham Greene whom I heard at Brussels evoking, before thousands of Belgian Catholics, and in the presence of a dreaming apostolic nuncio, the last pope of a totally dechristianized Europe, standing in line at the commissary, dressed in a spotted gabardine, and holding in his hand, on which still shone the Fisherman's ring, a cardboard valise.

That is to say that this book is addressed providentially to a generation that the absurdity of a crazy world is clutching by the throat. To the young contemporaries of Camus and Sartre, desperate prey to an absurd liberty, Graham Greene will reveal, perhaps, that this absurdity is in truth only that of boundless love.

The message is addressed to believers, to the virtuous, to those who do not doubt their merit and who have ever present in their minds several models of holiness, with the proper technic for attaining the various steps in the mystical ascension. It is addressed in particular to Christian priests and laymen, especially to writers who preach the cross but of whom it is not enough to say they are not crucified. A great lesson given to those obsessed with perfection, and those scrupulous people who split hairs over their shortcomings, and who forget that, in the last day, according to the word of Saint John of the Cross, it is on love that they will be judged.

Dear Graham Greene to whom I am attached by so many bonds, and first of all by those of gratitude (since thanks to you, my books to-day find the same warm reception in England that they received in my own country, at the time that I was a happy young author), how pleasant it is for me to think that France, where your work is already loved, is going to discover, thanks to that great book, *The Power and the Glory*, its true meaning. That state which you describe, which tracks down the last priest and assassinates him, is indeed the very one we see arising under our eyes. It is the hour of the Prince of this world, but you paint him without hatred. Even the executioners, even your chief of police is marked by you with a sign of mercy; they search for truth; they believe, like our communists, they have found it and are serving it—that truth which demands the sacrifice of consecrated creatures. Darkness covers all the earth you describe, but what a burning ray crosses it! Whatever happens, we know we must not be afraid; you remind us that the inexplicable will be explained and that there remains a grating to be put up against this absurd world. Through you, we know the adorable limit to the liberty that Sartre grants to men; we know that a creature loved as much as we are has no other liberty than that of refusing that love, to the degree to which it has made itself known to him and under the appearances it has been pleased to assume.

INDEX

Abratès, 80
Alceste, 16, 47, 48
Allart, Hortense, 63
Altuna, 36
Anet, Claude, 37
Angela of Foligno, Saint, 73
Angélique, Mother, 3
Anthony, St., 90
Argan, 11
Armance, 42
Armande, 12-14, 22, 23
Arnolphe, 15
Arnoux, Mme., 91, 99, 104
Attis, 75
Aziyadé, 106

Ball, The, 123
Balzac, 77-84
Baron, 22, 23
Barrès, Maurice, 4, 61, 62, 109-116
Baudelaire, 99
Bayle, 2
Béjart, Armande, 16
Béjart, Madeleine, 12
Benoît, Pierre, 121
Béranger, 95
Bernanos, 124, 125
Berthelot, 100
Bianchon, 78
Bibliothèque Rose, 81
Boileau, Abbé, 28
Bonald, 84, 115
Bonaparte, Napoleon, 61, 80, 84
Bossuet, 21, 43, 69, 124
Boullier, 28
Bourget, Paul, 77, 81, 113, 115
Bournisien, 103
Bouvard, 90, 93
Bovary, Charles, 91
Bovary, Emma, 91, 93, 100, 104
Brontë, 67
Brunschvicg, Léon, 1

Camus, 127
Capital, 114
Candide, 28
Caro, 71, 96
Castries, Duchess of, 80
Century of Louis XIV, The, 24
Centaur, The, 74

Chapelle, 14, 16
Charmettes, 44
Chesterton, 14, 28
Cicero, 39, 40, 92
Claudel, 117
Clermont, 5
Cocteau, Jean, 122
Coeur Simple, Un, 91, 99
Colet, Louise, 85, 86
Collin, Jacques, 80
Commanville, Mme., 100
Condorcet, 28
Confessions, 33, 34, 41, 46, 47, 49, 52
Coppée, François, 71
Coralie, 83
Count d'Orgel's Ball, 120, 121
Country Doctor, The, 81
Cybele, 51, 70, 74, 75

Daudet, 95
d'Argental, 27
d'Aurevilly, Barbey, 68, 70, 73, 74, 76
de Beaumont, Mme., 44, 63
de Beauséant, Viscountess, 78, 73
de Berny, 83
de Castries, Duchess, 80, 83
de Chateaubriand, François, 45, 46, 61-65, 115
de Chateaubriand, Mme., 61
de Chenonceaux, Mme., 33
d'Epinay, Mme., 32, 33, 48
de Festaud, Mme., 78
de Francueil, Mme., 31, 32, 35, 37
de Guérin, Eugénie, 66-76
de Guérin, Maurice, 51, 66-76
d'Houdetot, Mme., 32
de la Morvonnais, Hippolyte, 74
de Langeais, Duchess, 83
de Lastic, Count, 32
de Lisieux, Thérèse, 67
de Maistre, Baroness, 70, 71, 74
de Maistre, Joseph, 75, 84, 116
de Maupassant, 107
de Méré, Chevalier, 3
de Nucingen, Delphine, 78, 82, 83
d'Orgel, Mahaut, 123

de Poitevin, Alfred, 85-87
de Pommereu, Marchioness, 88
de Rastignac, Eugène, 78, 80, 82, 84
de Restaud, Anastasie, 83
de Roannez, Duke, 3, 6
de Roannez, Mademoiselle 5, 7
de Rubempré, Lucien, 80
de Sacy, 7
de Saint-Cyran, 25
de Trailles, Maxime, 78, 79, 84
Devil in the Body, The, 120
de Warens, Mme., 32, 37, 38, 45, 57, 58
Dialogues, 41, 49
Diderot, 42, 47, 57
Disciple, 113
Discours sur les Passions del Amour, 3, 5
Divine Comedy, 104
Didon, 100
Donissan, Abbé, 125
Dostoyefsky, 102, 103
Don Juan, 23
Du Bos, Charles, 101
du Camp, Maxime, 87, 95
Dupouey, 119

Eberhardt, Isabelle, 106
Eliot, 102, 103
Émile, 53
Encyclopedists, 41
Endymion, 75
Enemy of the Laws, The, 109
Esther, 83
Eugénie Grandet, 78

Fénélon, 124
Fernandez, 12, 14, 15, 20, 21, 23
Fermat, 3
Fitz-James, 80
Flaubert, Caroline, 85
Flaubert, Gustave, 85-104
Fléchier, 5
Formont, 26, 27
Free Man, The, 62

Garden of Bérénice, 110
Garden on the Orontes, A, 111, 112

129

Genius of Christianity, 63
Genius of the Rhine, 110
Gide, André, 46, 80, 117-119
Girodet, 65
Goethe, 61
Goriot, 77-84
Goncourt, 98, 101
Greene, Graham, 124-128
Grimm, 42, 57
Guyon, Mme., 45

Hamlet, 115
Hânem, Rachionk, 88
Harpagon, 23
Harnack, 7
Hommais, 102, 103
Human Comedy, The, 77, 78, 80-84
Huysmans, 99, 102

Immoralist, The, 119
Inquest into the Countries of the Levant, An, 111

Jacob, Max, 119, 122
Jammes, 117
Jesuits, 124
Johannot, Tony, 74
Joubert, 115
Julie, 98
Justin, 102

Labre, Benoît-Joseph, 44, 45
La Bruyère, 91, 115
Lacordaire, 45, 68, 124
Lafcadio, 118, 119
La Fontaine, 48
Lagneau, 115
Lamartine, 62
Lamennais, 45, 75, 124
La Polonaise, 80
La Rochefoucauld, 115
Lasserre, Pierre, 1, 6
la Tour, 46
Lemaître, Jules, 43, 59
Le Play, 115
Levasseur, 42
l'Homme libre, 8, 62
Loisy, 7
Lost Illusions, 80
Loti, 105-108
Louis Lambert, 81
Louis XVIII, 62
Lucretius, 20, 40
Lulli, 15
Luther, 39

Machiavelli, 114
Madame Bovary, 86, 90
Mademoiselle de la Ferté, 121
Malraux, 115
Marcus Aurelius, 92
Maréchal, 32
Marion, 31, 41
Maritain, Jacques, 36, 44
Marsays, 84
Marx, 114
Mathilde, Princess, 97

Maupertuis, 27
Mélicerte, 22
Mémoires d'outre-tombe, 64
Mérimée, 118
Michelet, 93, 94, 100
Michonneau, 81
Misanthrope, The, 16
Miser, 16
Molière, 11-23, 26
Morand, 122
Montherlant, 112, 115
My Heart Laid Bare, 99

Narcissus, 119
Nasie, 79
Nietzsche, 45, 46, 49, 61, 79, 80, 84
Nouvelle Héloïse, 33
Novalis, 113

Octave, 42
Oedipus, 115
Orgon, 11, 12, 14, 58
Other Side of Contemporary History, The, 81

Pascal, Blaise, 1-11, 13-19, 22, 24-26, 28, 29, 50, 104, 108, 115, 121
Pascal, Jacqueline, 3, 6, 8, 13
Pécuchet, 90-93
Périer, Marguérite, 4, 6, 7, 9, 15
Père Goriot, 77
Père-Lachaise, 83
Personality, 20
Pensées, 24, 27
Pensées et Opuscules, 1
Phèdre, 116
Philosophical Letters, 26
Pieta, 68
Polyeuctus, 6, 72
Porée, Father, 24
Poitou, 6
Power and the Glory, The, 124, 127
Prayer for the good use of illnesses, 6
Promenade, 57
Proust, Marcel, 4, 5, 14, 21, 46, 49, 80, 113
Provinciales, 26
Prudhomme, 92

Radiguet, Raymond, 120-123
Ramuncho, 106, 107
Remarks, 26
Remembrance of Things Past, 21
Renan, Abbé Ernest, 1, 6, 7, 64, 92, 93, 100
Reveries, 39, 41, 46, 54, 57
Reveries of a Solitary Wanderer, The, 49, 51, 59, 60
Revue hebdomadaire, 110
Revue des Deux Mondes, 74
Récamier, Mme., 64

Rimbaud, Arthur, 1, 8, 61
Rivière, Jacques, 75
Robespierre, 33
Rolland, Romain, 46
Fousseau, Jean-Jacques, 30, 60
Ruysbroeck, 55

Sailor, 105
Sainte-Beuve, 5, 20, 26, 33, 94, 97, 98, 100
Sainte-Perrine, 97
Salammbô, 90, 92
Salust, 40
Sand, George, 74
Sartre, 115, 127, 128
Sanson, 33
Savoy, Vicar of, 44, 55, 56
Schahabarim, 94
Sganarelle, 12, 15
Singlin, 5, 13, 94
Social Contract, The, 53
Socrates, 44, 119
Soubirous, Bernadette, 45
Spinoza, 95
Stalin, 62
Stendahl, 42, 117, 118
Strait Gate, The, 119
Strauss, 7
Sun of Satan, 125
Swann's Way, 46
Sylphide, 63

Tacitus, 39
Tartuffe, 11, 23, 58
Terence, 39
Their Faces, 112
Theresa, Saint, 90
Thérèse, 42, 43, 45
Thibaudet, 99
Three Reformers, 36
Three Tales, 99, 104
Tolstoi, 103
Toulié, Father, 24
Tournemine, Father, 24, 27
Two Pigeons, 6

Under the Eyes of the Barbarians, 109, 110

Vautrin, 79-81
Vauvenargues, 108
Veuillot, Louis, 124
Verlaine, 20
Vie de Rancé, 64
Vigny, 51
Villèle, 62
Virgil, 39
Voltaire, Arouet, 8, 24-29, 39, 43, 49, 94, 96

Wilde, Oscar, 20
Wintzenreid, 38

Yves, 106, 107

Zarathustra, 84
Zola, 81, 95, 98, 101, 102, 104, 107